# DEDICATION.

TO THE

## CHAIRMAN AND FEUARS

OF THE

## TOWN OF PATHHEAD.

GENTLEMEN,

The following Historical Sketches of the town of Pathhead and Vicinity have been prepared with considerable care. And having spent a long life in the midst of you, forty years of which I have been officially engaged in the business of the Feuars, and having largely shared in your sympathies and friendship, I feel much pleasure in dedicating to you this Volume; and trust that, in its perusal, you will be interested and gratified in contrasting the things which *were* with the things which *are*—the past with the present—the old with the new.

I am,

GENTLEMEN,

Your old neighbour and fellow-townsman,

ROBERT BRODIE.

PATHHEAD, *Sept.* 1863.

# HISTORICAL SKETCHES

OF

# PATHHEAD AND VICINITY.

BY

## ROBERT BRODIE,

CLERK TO THE FEUARS.

This facsimilie reprint of

HISTORICAL SKETCHES
OF
PATHHEAD AND VICINITY

First Published in 1863

is
*Published By*

Kirkcaldy District Council
Leisure and Direct Services Division
Kirkcaldy District Libraries
East Fergus Place
Kirkcaldy, KY1 1XT

*Printed by*
Cordfall Ltd., 041332 4640

# CONTENTS.

# PREFATORY NOTICE.

In sending forth the following pages to the reading public, the writer has to acknowledge with gratitude the cordial support which he has received from friends in this locality, both high and low. While a very few individuals have declined furnishing him with what information it may have been in their power to give regarding the topics introduced into this little work, *a large majority* of those to whom he applied kindly and promptly aided him in his endeavours to obtain suitable materials for constructing it ; and his wishes in this respect have even in some instances been anticipated. He has also to thank heartily several individuals who have kindly furnished him both with ancient and modern works, from which he has also quoted, with advantage, more or less.  And he concludes this notice with remarking, that while he has had a greater amount of labour in making search for suitable matter to fill up his little book than many are apt to suppose, he will not have to regret this as labour lost, if by its circulation it should minister to the instruction or amusement of his townsmen, or if it should only be of use to some future historian who may possess greater talent, or have more time at command than himself.

The author regrets very much that severe bodily indisposition has prevented him from giving the work that careful revision which otherwise he would have given it. And he trusts that the reader will kindly bear with him in this.

# HISTORICAL SKETCHES OF PATHHEAD AND VICINITY.

## INTRODUCTION.

DUNNIKIER proper, the estate on which the town of Pathhead stands, is bounded on the east by St Clairtown and the arable lands belonging to the Earl of Rosslyn; on the north, by the farm of Carberry, also the property of the Earl of Rosslyn; on the west, by the farm of Smeaton, the lands formerly of Halkhead Mills, now Braehead, and the Holmes; and on the south, by the sea flood. It appears to have originally consisted of two farms, the Nethertown and the Overtown. The former designation is not in use now; but it must have been used in former times, previous to feus being granted on the estate, for the term "Overtown" has no meaning taken by itself; it is a relative term. In some old documents it is termed "The Overtown of Dunnikier;" in others, "Over Dunnikier." There might have been some small patches of the estate which were not included in these two farms; but we have no doubt that these were its principal divisions. The farm-house of the Nethertown was, probably, that house at the east end of the Nether Street, standing back from the line of the rest of the houses, which was lately occupied as the post office.

The name, "Dunnikier," has probably a reference to its being a Roman or a Danish station in past ages. The literal signification of the word is, we believe, "the fortified hill," or, "the hill of the fort;" *Dun* signifying a hill or eminence of any kind, and *Keir*, a station. There are in various parts of Scotland, and, particularly, in Perthshire, a number of eminences which are termed Keirs; and, as the term is unquestionably not of Latin but of Celtic origin, it might have been applied to Roman or Danish stations indiscriminately. For, while it has been said that the Romans had a station at Carberry, it has also been asserted that the Danes landed in the neighbourhood of Dysart in 874, and fought a battle near Gallatown; but, as this is a matter of comparatively trifling importance, we leave it for our readers to judge of it for themselves.

## SITUATION AND GENERAL DESCRIPTION OF THE TOWN OF PATHHEAD.

The town of Pathhead stands upon the southern extremity of the estate of Dunnikier. It is bounded on the east by St Clairtown, from which it is separated by a hollow, through which flows the Rymalton burn. This hollow has been raised considerably in some places, particularly where it intersects the Nether and Mid streets, as will be seen at once by looking at the adjacent buildings; and the burn, or ditch, as it may rather be termed, is covered over now, its whole length, down to the sea-beach. The town is bounded on the south by the sea flood; on the west, by the Holmes and the lands of Halkhead Mills, now Brae-

head; and on the north, by the arable lands of Dunnikier.   The streets are parallel with the sea-beach, and,
considering all circumstances, are remarkable for their
regularity; much more so, indeed, than almost any
old town of its size which we remember to have seen.
While the town itself has a gentle rise from south to
north, the roads that lead from it to the sea-beach are
very steep; and, in the western half of the town, the
gardens overhang the sea at high water, the rocks
being quite precipitous in that quarter.   The situation
of the town is thus very high; perhaps it is the highest
of all the numerous towns that stud the southern coast
of Fife.   But, high as its position is, it is very evident
that it was at one time covered with the sea.   Yellow
and red sand, which has at one time or other formed part
of a sea-beach, is to be found to a considerable depth
over all the town.   Thus, the time has been when a
coal-laden sloop might have sailed up its eastern side
as far as the foot of the Broad Wynd, and a modern
first-rate man-of-war might have found water to float
her nearly up to the Panney Bridge.   Some of my
readers may be disposed to smile at this idea; but it
is a *fact* which they may easily prove for themselves.
It must be in the recollection of many, that, some
forty years ago, the skeleton of a whale was found at
Airth, not many miles from Stirling, and which, we
believe, was taken to the museum in the University of
Edinburgh.   Whether, then, the sea has sunk in this
quarter, or the land has emerged from it, we leave geo-
logists to determine; but the fact is incontrovertible,
that the whole site of the town of Pathhead was at
one time covered by the sea at high water.

Since writing the above, I have seen the *Edinburgh
Evening Courant* of March 3, 1863, in which is an

account of the Edinburgh Royal Society, from which I
quote the following : " The Rev. Thomas Brown gave in
a paper on ' A Clay Deposit, with Fossil Arctic Shells,
recently observed in the Basin of the Forth, similar to
the Glacial Beds of the Clyde.' Mr Brown, in the course
of his remarks, said, that the nature of the shells indicated that, since the period when they were alive,
*there must have been a rise of land of about three hun-
dred feet ;* and they also indicated a climate at that
time not less severe than Iceland or Greenland. Among
the shells found in this deposit, there was not, he
observed, one species which is not found alive at present in the Arctic seas, and a majority of the shells
nowhere else. He believed, therefore, that the group
was an Arctic group, and indicated an Arctic climate.

## STREETS AND ROADS.

The three principal streets stretch across the whole
breadth of the estate of Dunnikier at this spot, so that
the town cannot be extended any farther to the east
or to the west. The Nether Street is the nearest to
the sea. It, as well as the Mid Street, was formerly
paved with whin stones gathered from the land, or
round granite bullets which came from Aberdeen. The
manner in which these stones, the hardest and most
durable we have seen, found their way to this place,
was simply this :—In former times, coals and salt were
taken from Dysart to many places, and Aberdeen
among the rest ; and as the northern counties of Scotland had no grain, or anything else to give in return,
as they have now, the vessels which carried these com-
modities to the north were under the necessity of taking

quantities of stones for ballast every trip they made. We shall just give two illustrations of the manner in which the streets of our town were paved in old times:—

"Dunnikier, the eight day of October 1737 years. Mr James Oswald, and Thomas Grieg, sen., his baillie, enacts and ordaines, that the Over Wynd, in the middle of the town, and the wynd at the east end of the town twixt Walter Brydie's houses and Alexander Philp's houses, be casawayed; and for that effect, ordaines such heritors and inhabitants within Dunnikier to send out a man, for the space of a day each, for gathering of stones, and putting them in heaps where they can be most conveniently had; and ordaines such heritors and inhabitants as have horses to caw s$^d$ stones, when gathered, with their horses and slades, and lay the same down at said wynds; and for defraying the expences of laying thereof, the Laird of Dunnikier and his baillie, ordaines, that each heritor pay two shillings Scots for each ruid of ground he or she is heritor of, and so proportionally; and that the same be payed to such collector as shall be afterwards nominated; and to which enactment and ordinance the hail heritors present consent."

It does not appear, however, that the foregoing enactment was carried out in regard to the East Wynd, now Water Wynd.

Again—

"Dunnikier, the tenth day of November 1738 years. Dunnikier and his baillie, w$^t$ consent of a great many of the heritors, agrees that the vennels in the town be cassawayed, particularly the Mid Vennel, (Flesh Wynd, we suppose;) and in defraying the expences of cawing of stones and sand, and paying the cassawlayers, do hereby enact and agree that the heritors within the town pay three shills. Scots for each ruid, and each tenant, that are not heritors, pay twelve pennies Scots ; and appoints David Whyte for the south-east quarter, James Anderson for the south-west, Alex. Hardie for north-west, and David Thomson for north-east, for collectors ; and the officer to go with them.''

But to return to the Nether Street. It was causewayed, in the manner above stated, equally with the vennels and wynds. But in the year 1828, the Turnpike Road Trustees having adopted the Nether Street as a part of the turnpike road leading from Burntisland to Cupar, &c., lifted the whole of the causewaying in the street, and paved it with square stones. They also removed all the outside stairs, and made a footpath on the north side of the street, and, moreover, took off four or five feet in breadth from the east corner of the garden belonging to Mr John Thomson. These alterations made a very great improvement in the street, much to the comfort and convenience of passengers, and was well worth the large sum of money which it cost.

Leading from the Nether Street to the westward is the Path. We cannot now state precisely when the present Path was made, but it was some little time previous to 1779. Before that, the road to Kirkcaldy was by the old Path. It went from the Mid Street, on the south side of the burying-ground, and on the south side of Braehead House, and then by a gradual sweep down a natural hollow, until it came to the bridge. It must have been a very steep road, far more so than the present Path. This is the only road by which communication is held between Pathhead and Kirkcaldy, and is consequently much frequented at all hours of the day, and, we may add, night also. Indeed, we do not believe that there is, in all the Kirkcaldy trust district, a road on which there is so much traffic of horses, carriages, and pedestrians; but, strange to say, there is not a more inconvenient road in all the district. It is steep, narrow, and crooked; and after dark, notwithstanding the number of lamps erected, it is very dangerous. *There is not a bit of footpath on it.* We are very sorry to have it to chronicle, that there has been no attempt made to improve it by the road trustees. All the improvement which has been made on it during this century, is the slice which was taken off Mr Thomson's garden, at the top of it, and the making of a water-channel on the south side. We admit that it cannot be made what it is desirable it should be; but that is no reason why it should be neglected altogether. There was a good deal of interest taken in this matter by the public ten or eleven years ago. There was a good deal of discussion in the public prints called forth, and a public meeting was held in the Town Hall of Kirkcaldy, the Provost presiding. From this meeting a deputation was sent to the Road Trustees, at one of their public meetings, urging them to make a footpath; but after the Road-Surveyor had, by their orders, prepared a plan for widening the road and constructing a footpath, it came to nothing, for they said they had no funds. We shall merely remark farther, that it appears passing strange, that while there is one of the best paying tolls at the very spot, the money collected there is carried away to improve other pieces of road in the district, and nothing left for the improvement of the Path.

Jock's Road is a throughfare leading from the Path to the sea-beach. We have been informed that the

original Jock's Road commenced at the west end of the
Path houses, and went in a straight line to the south-
west corner of the Holmes, and received that name in
consequence of a mischievous boy named Jock, who
being pursued on account of having committed some
depredation, took this course in order to get out of the
reach of his pursuers. But, be that as it may, the
name was in course of time applied to the present
road. In the year 1804, the Messrs Dougal having
made a purchase of the Holmes, in the first place
erected a sea-wall on the south, and then proceeded to
repair and build up the wall on the north side along
the Path, with the full intention of shutting up Jock's
Road from being used as a thoroughfare to the sands by
the inhabitants of Pathhead. This proceeding on the
part of the Messrs Dougal roused up the feuars of
Pathhead to defend their right of way to the sands in that
direction. They at first attempted to get up a subscription among the inhabitants of the town, in order
to defend their rights from the encroachments of the
Messrs Dougal; but the subscription being a very poor
one, utterly inadequate for carrying the case into Court,
they unanimously came to the resolution of taking a
portion of the profits of the Muir for that purpose. It
was very fortunate for the feuars that their little
farm was by this time leaving a little profit after paying all expenses, else they would have been in a very
poor predicament. The Court of Session being applied
to, gave an interlocutor in favour of the feuars, purporting that they had an undoubted right to pass down
to the sands in that direction, but that the road must
be so constructed as to interfere as little as possible
with the Messrs Dougal's property. These gentlemen,
finding themselves baulked in their purpose of shutting

up the road, and the feuars urging them to carry out
the decree of the Court, proposed, one after another,
several parts of their property where they were willing
to allow a road to be constructed. But none of the
routes proposed being accepted by the feuars, all of
them being very steep and inconvenient, they, in the
year 1809, made application to the Court to compel
the Messrs Dougal to make the road in terms of the
interlocutor ; insisting, at the same time, on being put
in possession of the road which they had been in the
habit of using for a long time previous. It fortunately
happened that Lord Newton, before whom the case
was called at that time, came over to Fife on a visit
to Mr Ferguson of Raith. He embraced the opportunity
of visiting the spot personally, coming in that gentleman's carriage, and settled the road as it now is. The
*upper* half of the road is precisely that which the
feuars contended for from the beginning, but the lower
half goes further south than it did before, but it is quite
as good as the former termination, the Messrs Dougal
having been ordered by the Court to cut the rocks,
and make the road passable in the new direction. We
may further remark that, from the time when the road
was secured to the public by law to the year 1855, the
upper half of it was fully eight feet in breadth, being
so constructed by former proprietors for their own
convenience last century, and the lower half was four
feet, but in consequence of some alterations being
made in the vicinity, in the above-mentioned year, the
present proprietors of the Holmes made the whole
road of a uniform breadth of 6 feet, and built a pro-
tection wall on the west side of it. This lawsuit cost
the feuars of Pathhead the sum of £73, 7s. 8d., whereof
the Court adjudged the Messrs Dougal to pay £26, 13s.,

but whether that sum was ever paid to the feuars or their agents, we have not been able to ascertain.

But, while the above-mentioned road could not by any means be converted into a cart-road, there is a road of this description at the foot of the Path, and close on the east side of the toll-bar. It is fourteen feet in breadth, and has always been claimed by the feuars as their property ; and as such they keep it in repair. It is very convenient for carrying down rubbish from the town, or bringing up sand, or stones, or sea-weed. There have been several attempts made, however, to deprive them of it. Somewhere about the year 1821 the proprietors of the distillery in the neighbourhood, in enclosing their property on the south side of the turnpike-road, so extended a wall which they had built there, as to all intents and purposes shut up the road. In consequence of this the feuars sent a deputation to these gentlemen to request them to take down part of the wall which they had built, in order that the road might be restored to the public. The right of the feuars was admitted, having been secured to them at some former period by the Sheriff of Fife, and a promise of granting their request was given, but it was not fulfilled until a second application was made to them, when they took down six feet of the wall, and thus the road was reopened. We may also add, that the tacksman of the toll-bar, a few years ago, attempted to lay toll on all carts going up or down this road, but a public-spirited feuar in Pathhead took the matter before the Sheriff, who gave a decision in his favour. Therefore, no toll can be legally charged for the use of this road now.

We now turn to the Nether Street again, and remark that there is a thoroughfare, termed the Vennel, which leads from about the middle of the street down to the sea-beach. In former times there were several lanes or passages in the town, which were termed Vennels, but these thoroughfares have received other designations now, and the term Vennel is exclusively applied to the road we are now describing. It is, of course, very steep, and formerly it was causewayed from head to foot with the same kind of stones as were to be seen in other parts of the town. But, of late years, it has been much improved ; the dirty water, which runs from the street through it, being entirely covered over, and steps being made in different parts of it, for the ease and convenience of passengers. These improvements have been made, from time to time, at the expense of the feuars, Philp's Institution, and private subscription.

At the east end of the Nether Street is the New Road, which, like the Vennel, leads down to the sea-beach. It is the boundary betwixt Pathhead and St Clairtown in that quarter. It was made at the sole expense of Sir James St Clair, in the year 1800. The feuars of Pathhead have assisted in repairing it, in several instances, since that. The dirty water there, too, is covered over entirely ; and although it is very steep, yet it is very convenient, not only for the inhabitants of St Clairtown, but also for those who reside in the eastern parts of Pathhead, when they wish to go to the sands.

Leading east from the Nether Street, and nearly in a line with it, is the road that leads to Dysart. The *old* road was particularly straight and level, for about four-fifths of its length, from the west end. It had a footpath of about four feet broad on the side of it. After it reached the Earl of Rosslyn's garden, it went along its south side, winding to the north, and descend-

ing somewhat abruptly to the top of the Hellpot Wynd.
Near the west end of this road, and a few yards to the
north, surrounded by a wall, stood *the three trees,* as
they were called, although, we believe, there were only
two of them.   Various legends have been circulated in
reference to the reason of their being planted ; but as
none of them can be relied on as being founded on fact,
we refrain from repeating them.   The present road to
Dysart was made about 1820.   It is considerably wider
than the old one, and it has a much broader footpath,
but it has a considerable rise from both ends.

The Mid Street stands next to the Nether Street.
Indeed, these two streets constituted the whole town
of Pathhead previous to about 1720.   Before that
period they bore respectively the names of the Nether-
gate and the Midgate.   It was formerly paved with
flattish or round stones, like the Nether Street, as we
have already said, and, like it, too, was encumbered
with outside stairs.   The stairs, since 1800, have
been reduced in number sixteen or seventeen ; and, in
1849, the feuars lifted the whole of the causewaying
from the West Wynd to the Water Wynd, and laid the
middle of it with square stones, and the sides with the
best of the old stones.   A kerb stone was also laid
down, and a new water channel made on both sides of
the street.   The expense was borne partly by private
subscription, and partly by the feuars' public income.
The subscription amounted to £70, 3s., and the feuars
furnished the remainder of the sum required—£107,
3s. 6d. ; total, £177, 6s. 6d.   In the following year,
the feuars voted £3 to assist in removing the " *Muckle
Lum.*"   This was a very unsightly piece of masonry
attached to the front of a house on the north side of
the street, being much larger and clumsier than an

outside stair, and taking up nearly the whole breadth of the footpath.

In 1860, the feuars, at an expense of £146, finished the east end of the Mid Street, not merely paving it like the rest of the street, but also raising it at the hollow, and also laying down a 12-inch tile-drain, from the foot of the Water Wynd eastward to the Rymalton, or march-burn, making it considerably more steep than the old stone drain had been. The Broad Wynd, which is the boundary at that spot between Pathhead and St Clairtown, was also paved, and a kerb stone laid down on both sides; this was the first time it had been paved. Expense of the wynd included in the above sum.

It is proper to state here that the feuars have been at considerable expense in improving the "Chief's Close" and "Wemyss' Close," both being thoroughfares leading from Nether Street to Mid Street. And moreover, the feuars were, in 1858, at the *sole* expense of laying Bogie's Wynd, leading from Mid Street to Back Street, with square stones, the whole breadth of it, and also half of the expense of Arbroath pavement for the footpath on each side,—the proprietors in the wynd paying the other half. A very important improvement has been lately carried out in Flesh Wynd. An underground drain has been laid down the whole length, the greater part of which is *built* of brick, with Gallatown pavement for bottom and cover, the remainder is a 12-inch drain pipe, and goes the length of the foot of Bogie's Wynd, where there are two grates placed to carry the water into the drain. The whole causewaying has been taken up, and the wynd paved from kerb to kerb, the whole length, with square stones. But there is another thoroughfare con-

nected with Mid Street which must not be forgotten.
We refer to the West Wynd, but as this wynd happens
to be a part of the statute-labour road in this quarter,
the trustees paid part of the expense of improving it.
This improvement was conjoined with the laying of
kerb and channel in the west half of Back Street. The
whole work cost £104—whereof the road trustees
paid £30, the feuars the remainder. Back Street,
West Wynd, and from the foot of West Wynd to the
Path, being part of the statute-labour road, the improvement consisted in paving it with square stones
the whole breadth, laying down a 9-inch tile-drain its
whole length, and making a small footpath upon its east
side. The tile-drain was carried west from the foot of
the wynd, along the Mid Street (increased in bore to 12
inches) to the head of Plantin Wynd, where it enters
into a stone drain previously constructed there. That
little portion of Mid Street is not quite finished yet.
The feuars voted some time ago that kerb stones should
be laid down, and new water channels constructed on
both sides, provided the Statute-labour Trustees paid
half the expense. It is to be hoped that this little bit
of improvement will be carried out shortly.

The Back Street now demands our brief consideration. Feus began to be granted in this street in 1720,
or perhaps earlier, but it was not all feued until 1737.
It should here be noticed, however, that a thoroughfare,
called the "Mill Vennel," leading all the way from Dysart
to the mill at the bridge of Invertiel, commonly called
the West Mill, passed along where the Back Street now
stands. This road existed at a very early period, indeed no one can tell how early. In its original state
it was merely a footpath of sufficient breadth to allow
a man to walk along with a sieve under his arm. Every

feuar on the north side of the Mid Street, both in Pathhead and St Clairtown, had the privilege of having a
door in his north wall, in order to have communication
with this road. Several of these are still to be seen in
the Back Street. But although " *Mill Vennel* " was
the proper name of this thoroughfare, and properly
pointed out its peculiar use, namely, to allow the inhabitants of Dysart, St Clairtown, and Pathhead to
pass along to the mill at Invertiel Bridge without
entering into any of the streets in these localities, yet
in Pathhead district it was always termed the Back-i'-
dikes ; and, moreover, after the Back Street was built,
and many years thereafter, *it* went by the name of
Back-i'-dikes, and even for some years in this present
century it still retained that old-fashioned appellation.
Back Street was a term which was never made use of ;
the writer has a personal knowledge of this circumstance. We cannot at present say at what time the
Back Street became a statute-labour road, but it is a
certain fact that a number of years of this century had
passed before it was macadamised, or a water channel
made on the south side of it, although the one on the
*north* side had been formed in the latter part of last
century. Sixty years ago it was in such a bad state
that often in winter it was only at certain spots that a
foot passenger could get across ; but now it is kept in
good order by the trustees. Great improvements have
been made on it of late, partly at the expense of the
road trustees and partly at the expense of the feuars.
Thus, in the years 1856 and 1857, the old water channels were taken up and new ones constructed the whole
length of the street on both sides, and kerb stones to
correspond were added. And further, since that improvement was completed, another has been effected in

the laying down of Arbroath pavement on the north footpath, 3 feet in breadth, so that, connected with portions of pavement which had been previously laid down by feuars in front of their own properties, there is now an excellent and clean-looking footpath the whole length of the street. This last improvement has been effected by private subscription and by the public funds of the feuars in equal proportions. But the south footpath of this street has not been neglected. Although not privileged with pavement, it is kept in good order by having channel laid on it from time to time. Altogether, there has been a wonderful improvement in the appearance of this street since the beginning of this century. Then it was in a very bad state, as we have already said, but now it is smooth and clean, safe and commodious, for horses, carriages, and pedestrians. There is a remark which we feel ourselves bound to make here, but it has a reference to all the three streets which we have been endeavouring to describe, namely, that at the beginning of this century, and from time immemorial, for anything that we know to the contrary, there were dunghills of the most offensive description to be seen here and there, lying close to the walls of the houses, under the windows and by the sides of the doors. These were most injurious to the health of the inhabitants. We are happy to have it in our power to record now that all such nuisances have been swept away for several years back, and the consequence has been that the health of the people has improved. And to this it may be added, that now there is a regular system of cleaning in *all* the streets —a sweeper being constantly engaged, and the sweepings *carried away daily*.

Birrel Street is the last thoroughfare which we shall

have to notice. It is a short street, parallel with the other streets, and lying contiguous to Back Street. It was built about the year 1790; but it was only in 1860 that it was macadamised, and the water channels properly finished. This improvement was made at the joint expense of the feuars, and the individual proprietors in the street.

Previous to the year 1822, the streets of Pathhead were in total darkness; but on July 5, that year, at the annual general meeting of feuars, it was unanimously resolved to light the streets with oil lamps; and, for that purpose, that lamps, globes, and lamp-irons should be purchased from the towns' funds, provided the inhabitants upheld oil, wicks, lamplighters' wages, and replace globes, if necessary—tenants and feuars alike. This resolution was carried into effect; the lamps were erected and lighted that year, and the two following years—the inhabitants giving a voluntary contribution for that purpose, and the feuars furnishing the remainder from their public funds. However, in the year 1825, the feuars, finding that the sum subscribed by the inhabitants was by far too small, they resolved that the lamps *should not be lighted that season*. A reaction took place the following year, 1826; for, in September, it was unanimously resolved, at a general meeting, to light the lamps that season wholly from the public funds. In 1834, the inhabitants of the parish of Dysart, having adopted two of the clauses of the Police Act for Scotland, which had been lately passed—namely, those which relate to cleaning and lighting the streets—the feuars agreed to *lend* the lamps to the Police Commissioners for the use of the town. The same year the feuars resigned into the hands of the said Commissioners their superintendence of the cleaning of the streets. The street lamps were first lighted with gas the same year.

There are scarcely any buildings in the town of Pathhead worthy of being noticed in this little work. Nine-tenths of the houses are old, or, at least, look old. Almost the whole of them, however, have had their thatched roofs removed, and replaced with tile ones. While, before 1800, only two of the old houses had been taken down and replaced with respectable ones, there has been a number of them removed since, and their places filled up with very superior ones. There is only one *old* house in the whole town which is respectable in its appearance; that is the one built by John Watson, proprietor of the estate of Dunnikier, in 1692, in the west end of the Nether Street, now in the possession of Mr John Thomson. Mr Watson's initials, and those of his wife, Euphan Orrock, are carved on the front, and also the date of its erection. It has been very much improved of late years, at considerable expense. Philp's school stands in the same street—a very plain, comfortable-looking building, with a steeple seventy-five feet high, having a clock on its front. There is a spacious play-ground in front of the school, with a shed for the convenience of the scholars in rainy weather. A few yards west stands Nairn's floor-cloth manufactory. This is a building of an immense size, four storeys high. It is nearly four-square, and has no fewer than one hundred and forty-six windows. It is said to be the only manufactory of the kind in Scotland. It furnishes employment for about one hundred persons, male and female. The town-hall stands between the Nether and Mid streets, near the east end of the town. It was erected in 1832, and the very first purpose to which it was applied was that of being a cholera hospital. It is not very large, being only 24 feet by 16 inside the walls. Underneath is a lock-up house, containing two cells and a dwelling-house for the police-constable. The whole building is very plain. It was erected at an expense of £157, whereof Sir John Oswald contributed £40, and the Earl of Rosslyn, £26—the feuars furnishing the remainder. Sir John, in giving his quota, stipulated for the exclusive use of a press, and also the use of the hall for holding courts, and drawing up the feu-duties. The Earl of Rosslyn has no interest in the *hall*, but merely gave his donation for the privilege of putting persons into the lock-up who might be apprehended in St Clairtown. In the east end of Birrel Street, there is a power-loom factory lately established. There is nothing remarkable in regard to its outward appearance. It is only one storey in height, with six narrow roofs. It is capable of containing one hundred looms, but as yet there are only fifty erected. It affords employment to about sixty individuals.

## THE BURYING GROUND.

On 31st July 1684, John Watson and Euphan Orrock, his wife, gave through George Flockhart, elder, to Magnus Porringer, wright in Dunnikier, for himself, and as procurator and attorney, for and in name of the hail inhabitants of the town and lands of Dunnikier, a piece of ground for a burying-place; of five ruids in breadth, each ruid six ells in breadth, and thirty-six ells in length; bounded on the east by the feu of John Paton; on the north by the lands of Dunnikier; on the west by the lands of Hawkhead Mills (now Brae-

head); and on the south by the high road.  It may
here be remarked, however, that the actual measurement of the ground does not correspond with the terms
of the grant; for there being more than one angle in
the whole burying-ground, the measurement of this
original piece is considerably short of thirty-six Scots
ells on the west side; but this deficiency is more than
made up on the east side.  Up to January 1707, the
ground was not enclosed; neither was there any record
kept of the interments, but there is undoubted evidence
to prove that interments *did* take place in it before
that period.  In the earliest records of the burying-
ground, there are references to former interments; such
as, for instance, a person is said to have been interred
in the grave of his father, when the actual interment
of that father is not to be found; but, moreover, and
still more to the point, there is a headstone in the
yard, which was erected by David Kinnear and Elisabeth Dawson, his wife, in 1699, and the first record
of interment on this stone is that of Margaret Durie,
mother of Elisabeth Dawson, who died September 11,
1696; and then follows, — Kinnear, 1697; — Kinnear, 1698.  It is probable that these two last were
young children of David Kinnear.  He died himself in
1715, although his interment is not recorded upon the
stone.

At the time we have already mentioned—namely,
January 1707—the majority of the inhabitants convened, and burdened themselves, and the other inhabitants of the town, with twelve shillings Scots for
each feuable ruid within the said town, payable by
each feuar; and eight shillings money foresaid, payable by each householder not being a feuar; which
money was to be applied for building and upholding a
dyke about the forementioned parcel of ground.  More-

over, they, finding the forementioned money not sufficient for the use and ends, therefore it was ordained and appointed, that, each person come to age, their burial shall cost eighteen shillings Scots for bell and grave ; and for each child, twelve shillings money foresaid—the one-half to him that rings the bell and makes the grave, and the other half to the hand of a public collector appointed by the inhabitants to that effect, and to be applied for the upholding of foresaid dyke. It was likewise thought fit, that whoever was pleased to order the bell to go three several times through the town, should pay two shillings money foresaid more, for the use of him that rings the bell allenarly.

In pursuance of these resolutions the inhabitants of Pathhead set themselves resolutely to enclose the burying-ground. Every one was taxed precisely in terms of the resolutions ; a book was purchased to answer for both cash and minute-book, and the names of all who paid the tax are recorded in the beginning of this book. The feuars are first in order, upwards of fifty in number, and it is seen at a glance how many feuing ruids each possess by the sum of money which he paid. The first name on the list is John Watson, late Laird of Dunnikier, £2, 18s., which shews that he possessed at that time nearly five feuing ruids. Next follows householders who were not feuars, to the number of a hundred and fifty or more. It appears that the dyke was originally built with stones and divots without any lime, except at the gate. There is none of the original standing now, except at the gate. The whole expense of dyke and gates appear to have been about £5, 7s. sterling.

A collector was, of course, appointed, and the accounts were examined annually by several of the feuars, and it would appear that the collectors were changed

annually for the first few years at least.   But in May
1719, we find the title " Collector " exchanged for
that of " Boxmaster," and, at that period, we find that
eight individuals were appointed to assist and advise
the boxmaster, as also to examine his receipts and disbursements at the end of the year.  Two of the number
were key-keepers.  On the box there were two locks,
diverse from each other, so that it could not be opened
without both the key-keepers being present.  There is
still a box belonging to the feuars, constructed on this
principle, and which was made as late as 1810, and
we believe that all benefit societies during the last
century and part of the present one, in this neighbourhood at least, had boxes of this kind ; and the preses
was consequently termed the *Boxmaster*, who merely
kept the box in his house, but could not open it.  Of
course, in the present day, when there are so many
banks established all over the country, the system is
entirely altered ; if a society has any funds to lay up,
they are as safe in a bank as being placed in a double-
locked box ; besides, on the former plan they will be
accumulating by the addition of the interest.  We may
just add here, that the individuals chosen to assist the
boxmaster, were sometimes termed his assistants, sometimes his auditors, and sometimes simply the aught
men.   They were chosen regularly from the different
quarters of the town ; thus, two from the east end of
the Nether Street, one from each side of the street, two
from the west half of the Nether Street, one from each
side of the street, and the same arrangement for the
Mid Street.  The Back Street was not then built.

On the 10th July 1740, Mr James Oswald, the then
proprietor of the estate of Dunnikier, granted, by
charter, eighteen ells of ground to be added to the

length of the original piece, viz. to David Whyte, and
other members of the Burial-yard Box, for the use and
behoof of the poor and indigent members of the said
box. It is very difficult to understand what is intended
by this peculiar phraseology, but we may just remark,
that this piece of ground was enclosed along with the
original piece, and has always been managed in the
same manner, and has been made use of precisely for
the same purpose, namely, for the interment of the
dead in Dunnikier, from its first grant until the present day. The cash and minute-book to which we
have already referred comes no farther down than
1757, the Boxmaster at that time being Thomas
Alison, whose brother James was killed by the falling
of the Cove in 1740. The writer has a distinct recollection of Thomas; he died in 179—. From 1757 we
have no account even of the names of the boxmasters
until 1793, where, in the charter of the Muir, we find
the name of the late Mr David Millie as filling that
office, and also the names of all the managers, as stated
in another section of this work. After 1793 there is
no account extant of the boxmasters until 1802, when
the late Mr Michael Duff was boxmaster; and his
name, and also the names of all the managers were
found inserted in a minute written on a loose piece of
paper, which was found lying in the charter-box, but
which is now pasted in the minute-book. This minute
was a very important one. It related exclusively to
the transfer of the old school-house from the original
subscribers to the feuars. There is thus no minute-
book from 1757 to 1802; and further, there is no
cash-book from 1757 to 1810. There can be no
doubt that the burial-yard accounts were kept in
some fashion during that long period, but they have

not come down to us. While we are speaking about books, it must be distinctly noticed that there has been a correct account of the interments kept from January 1707 to the present day. The first volume, reaching from that date to 1714, was unfortunately burnt, by accident no doubt. The first volume, which is in existence, reaches from 1714 to 1727, the next from 1727 to 1740, the next from 1740 to 1766, the next from 1766 to 1806, the next from 1806 to 1848, when the current volume commences. All these books are in the custody of the clerk. Moreover, the three first volumes, extending from 1714 to 1766, have been rebound, and the indexes recompiled a few years ago, so that the *whole* of the records down to the present time are now in good order. Any name that is wanted may be found without loss of time, which is not the case with other funeral registers in this neighbourhood which we have examined. The burial-yard officials in Pathhead began at the very first to keep their registers on a correct plan, with complete indexes, and the system has been uniformly adhered to ever since.

Before we proceed farther, we shall make two remarks regarding the management of the burial-yard box for the first fifty years. First, the managers never allowed themselves to get into debt, on the contrary, they had always some money on hand, however little. At one time, indeed, they had £50 Scots lent to a feuar, on a bill bearing interest. This money was called up, however, when a new pair of gates were going to be put up. And second, in numerous instances, and in various ways, they disposed of their surplus funds for the public good, or for the benefit of needy individuals. Thus, "October 2, 1724, pd. for reparations of the bridge £24.—November 30, 1733, delivered out of burial-yard box, by me, John Johnston, with advice of others, the sum of four pounds, nine shillings, to help the buchan fees this year, before these witnesses under subscribing, Thomas Greig, witness, Da. Thomson, witness.—28th February 1749, Given out to the use of setting doun the well in the West Quarter in the Nether-gate, by consent of the Managers of the Burying-yard Box, the sum of fourty shillings sterling." The common well was taken a deep interest in; it often had a share of the surplus funds. Sometime they gave a donation towards keeping it in repair, at other times they employed tradesmen and paid them themselves. There were, moreover, from time to time, small sums given to poor people to buy a pair of shoes, to buy a horse, &c.; and, in the greater number of instances, a few shillings Scots were given, without any definite object being mentioned. But, over and above all these applications of the public funds, there was the continually recurring item for putting away cripples, for which 2d. Scots were allowed each time. These individuals, after being carried from door to door by the inhabitants on their own hand-barrow, were at last carried on to Dysart or to Kirkcaldy, as the case might be, by people employed for the purpose. This practice of beggars being carried thus from door to door, and from town to town, was continued for some years in this century.

Some time in the latter half of last century, the dues of the burying-ground were lowered, entries being made 8s., feuars and non-feuars alike, and interments 6s., for adults as well as children. During that period also, the practice of examining the boxmaster's book and accounts was given up. Perhaps the smallness of the revenue led the managers to think it unnecessary.

But even after the year 1796, when the income of the farm was amalgamated with that of the burying-ground, still there was no auditing of books. At the annual meetings of the feuars, the receipts and disbursements for the past year were read by the clerk, and the committee for the ensuing year was chosen, until the year 1833, when auditors were appointed to examine the books and vouchers, and this practice has continued ever since. The last donation that was given from the burial-yard fund proper was in 1794, when £2 was voted towards building the subscription schoolhouse. A great improvement was made in the burying-ground in 1862, in levelling it, and placing the headstones in an orderly manner. It will be at once seen that there are no private rights in these two portions of ground we have been speaking about. Neither the committee nor any private individual can sell any portion of these grounds ; neither can any party rail in any part of them. The property belongs to the present generation of the inhabitants for the burying of their dead.

But we now proceed to state, that in the year 1828, at which period the burying-grounds, Nos. 1 and 2, as we may designate them, were deemed insufficient for the wants of an increasing population, the feuars purchased a garden that lay contiguous to the burying-ground, and took off about a fifth part of it, and added it to the old ground. After long consideration, it was resolved to draw up a proper plan of this new piece of ground, which was accordingly done, divided in 126 lots, each lot containing three grave-breadths, and to be sold for £1 the lot. A printed charter is given with each lot that is sold, giving the purchaser full power to use it for a burying-place for his family, or any person whom he may choose to admit into it. He may sell it to another party, or he may bequeath it to his heirs and successors; but if it is not claimed or made use of for forty years it reverts back to the feuars, who can sell it again. We may add here, that when a person pays entry-money to the old ground, it secures a burying-place for himself, his wife, and all his unmarried children, the entry being raised in 1831 to 2s. 6d.

INTERMENTS IN THE *WHOLE* BURYING-GROUND EACH YEAR, ENDING 31st DECEMBER.

| YEAR. | | INTERMENTS. | YEAR. | | INTERMENTS. |
|---|---|---|---|---|---|
| 1707, | ... | 33 | 1725, | ... | 29 |
| 1708, | ... | 20 | 1726, | ... | 24 |
| 1709, | ... | 23 | 1727, | ... | 32 |
| 1710, | ... | 43 | 1728, | ... | 32 |
| | | —— | 1729, | ... | 46 |
| | | 119 | 1730, | ... | 45 |
| | | —— | | | —— |
| Average of 4 years, | | 29¾ | | | 370 |
| | | | | | —— |
| 1711, | ... | 20 | Average, | | 37 |
| 1712, | ... | 22 | | | —— |
| 1713, | ... | 18 | 1731, | ... | 43 |
| 1714, | ... | 13 | 1732, | ... | 50 |
| 1715, | ... | 55 | 1733, | ... | 51 |
| 1716, | ... | 21 | 1734, | ... | 59 |
| 1717, | ... | 20 | 1735, | ... | 28 |
| 1718, | ... | 21 | 1736, | ... | 37 |
| 1719, | ... | 27 | 1737, | ... | 38 |
| 1720, | ... | 41 | 1738, | ... | 45 |
| | | —— | 1739, | ... | 50 |
| | | 258 | 1740, | ... | 49 |
| | | —— | | | —— |
| Average, | | 25$\frac{8}{10}$ | | | 450 |
| | | —— | | | —— |
| 1721, | ... | 34 | Average, | | 45 |
| 1722, | ... | 33 | | | |
| 1723, | ... | 40 | 1741, | ... | 54 |
| 1724, | ... | 55 | 1742, | ... | 52 |

| YEAR. | | INTERMENTS. | YEAR. | | INTERMENTS. |
|---|---|---|---|---|---|
| 1743, | ... | 36 | 1771, | | 48 |
| 1744, | ... | 36 | 1772, | ... | 85 |
| 1745, | ... | 26 | 1773, | ... | 45 |
| 1746, | ... | 27 | 1774, | ... | 41 |
| 1747, | ... | 61 | 1775, | ... | 49 |
| 1748, | ... | 31 | 1776, | ... | 46 |
| 1749, | ... | 69 | 1777, | ... | 40 |
| 1750, | ... | 46 | 1778, | ... | 30 |
| | | | 1779, | ... | 25 |
| | | 438 | 1780, | ... | 38 |
| | | | | | 447 |

Average,    $43\frac{8}{10}$

Average,    $44\frac{7}{10}$

| 1751, | ... | 55 | | | |
| 1752, | ... | 57 | 1781, | ... | 32 |
| 1753, | ... | 76 | 1782, | ... | 38 |
| 1754, | ... | 35 | 1783, | ... | 68 |
| 1755, | ... | 45 | 1784, | ... | 46 |
| 1756, | ... | 54 | 1785, | ... | 71 |
| 1757, | ... | 65 | 1786, | ... | 45 |
| 1758, | ... | 62 | 1787, | ... | 63 |
| 1759, | ... | 39 | 1788, | ... | 47 |
| 1760, | ... | 86 | 1789, | ... | 42 |
| | | | 1790, | ... | 69 |
| | | 574 | | | |
| | | | | | 521 |

Average,    $57\frac{4}{10}$

Average,    $52\frac{1}{10}$

| 1761, | ... | 43 | 1791, | ... | 42 |
| 1762, | ... | 60 | 1792, | ... | 51 |
| 1763, | ... | 45 | 1793, | ... | 53 |
| 1764, | ... | 52 | 1794, | ... | 97 |
| 1765, | ... | 48 | 1795, | ... | 58 |
| 1766, | ... | 47 | 1796, | ... | 52 |
| 1767, | ... | 48 | 1797, | ... | 52 |
| 1768, | ... | 48 | 1798, | ... | 52 |
| 1769, | ... | 27 | 1799, | ... | 65 |
| 1770, | ... | 71 | 1800, | ... | 51 |
| | | 489 | | | 573 |

Average,    $48\frac{9}{10}$

Average,    $57\frac{3}{10}$

| YEAR. | | INTERMENTS. | YEAR. | | INTERMENTS. |
|---|---|---|---|---|---|
| 1801, | ... | 75 | 1831, | ... | 76 |
| 1802, | ... | 62 | 1832, | ... | 73 |
| 1803, | ... | 44 | 1833, | ... | 55 |
| 1804, | ... | 42 | 1834, | ... | 35 |
| 1805, | ... | 48 | 1835, | ... | 33 |
| 1806, | ... | 37 | 1836, | ... | 30 |
| 1807, | ... | 42 | 1837, | ... | 45 |
| 1808, | ... | 47 | 1838, | ... | 41 |
| 1809, | ... | 53 | 1839, | ... | 39 |
| 1810, | ... | 36 | 1840, | ... | 55 |
| | | 486 | | | 482 |
| Average, | | $48\frac{6}{10}$ | Average, | | $48\frac{2}{10}$ |
| 1811, | ... | 35 | 1841, | ... | 60 |
| 1812, | ... | 30 | 1842, | ... | 47 |
| 1813, | ... | 29 | 1843, | ... | 49 |
| 1814, | ... | 51 | 1844, | ... | 65 |
| 1815, | ... | 53 | 1845, | ... | 41 |
| 1816, | ... | 37 | 1846, | ... | 43 |
| 1817, | ... | 32 | 1847, | ... | 74 |
| 1818, | ... | 44 | 1848, | ... | 72 |
| 1819, | ... | 59 | 1849, | ... | 67 |
| 1820, | ... | 57 | 1850, | ... | 37 |
| | | 437 | | | 555 |
| Average, | | $43\frac{7}{10}$ | Average, | | $55\frac{6}{10}$ |
| 1821, | ... | 45 | 1851, | ... | 37 |
| 1822, | ... | 40 | 1852, | ... | 54 |
| 1823, | ... | 55 | 1853, | ... | 50 |
| 1824, | ... | 46 | 1854, | ... | 57 |
| 1825, | ... | 42 | 1855, | ... | 68 |
| 1826, | ... | 52 | 1856, | ... | 44 |
| 1827, | ... | 44 | 1857, | ... | 52 |
| 1828, | ... | 48 | 1858, | ... | 42 |
| 1829, | ... | 55 | 1859, | ... | 57 |
| 1830, | ... | 44 | 1860, | ... | 49 |
| | | 471 | | | 510 |
| Average, | | $47\frac{1}{10}$ | Average, | | 51 |

1. It has been already stated that the Register

from January 1707 to August 1714, was burned; however, the numbers for that period have been recovered from the cash-book. These numbers may be considered pretty correct, with the exception of paupers, which, of course, are not recorded in the cash-book.

2. The greatest annual mortality was in 1794, when the number of interments was 97. The smallest annual mortality was in 1714, the numbers being 13. The greatest monthly mortality was in September 1794, the interments being 19. There have been a number of blank months through the whole period. The highest average number for ten years was from 1790 to 1800, being $59\frac{3}{10}$. The lowest average of ten years was from 1710 to 1720, when the number was $25\frac{8}{10}$. In general, where the number of interments are above the average, the increase is in children. We have tested this in regard to several years in last century. In regard to the year 1832, when cholera prevailed to such an alarming extent, it may be supposed that the numbers would be unprecedentedly large; but this was not the case, for in the previous year, when a number of fatal cases of dysentry were in this place, the number was greater. In 1831, the number of interments was 76; in 1832, 73.

3. That the rate of mortality is far lower now than it was a hundred years ago, must strike every attentive reader of these statistics. The population has at least been doubled, while the interments have very slightly increased, and even in the case of children perhaps have *decreased*. This speaks volumes in favour of vaccination and cleanliness in houses and in streets.

4. But, after all, the number of interments in Pathhead burying-ground does not afford a correct view of

the actual mortality in the town ; for while, on the one
hand, now and then there are inhabitants of the town
taken to other burying-grounds to be interred, there
are, on the other hand, a number of persons brought
every year from other districts to be interred here.
St Clairtown is the principal district from which these
strangers come. The St Clairtown burying-ground
came into use in the year 1756. In the five years
previous there were 5 persons brought from thence to
Pathhead to be interred, but in the five years previous
to 1856 there were 38. This great increase arises
undoubtedly from the great increase of population.
The first interment in this town from St Clairtown took
place on October 20, 1731, being a child of Thomas
Russel, hammerman. From that date to January 1,
1756, there were 40 interments from St Clairtown
in Pathhead burying-ground.

-----

## THE FARM.

Of course, in speaking of the farm now belonging to
the feuars of Pathhead, it is indispensable that we take
notice of its origin, and by what means it came into
their possession. These two ideas involve each other.
The privilege of the feuars, in regard to the Muir, dates
as far back as the year 1608. In that year, the
Honourable Robert Lundie granted liberty to the feuars
to " faul, dovett, claye, and querrell." It is not stated
from what part of the estate of Dunnikier these articles
were to be taken ; but in the oldest charters given after
that period, which we have been able to decipher, it is
expressly stipulated that the individual feuar to whom
the charter was granted should have the privilege of

" casting, winning, and away carrying stones and clay,
fail and divot, *from the Muir of Dunnikier*, for building
or repairing the houses built or to be built on his feu."
Notwithstanding, however, of this unconditional grant
of materials by several proprietors of Dunnikier to the
feuars, we find that in the year 1666, John Watson,
sen., commenced a lawsuit against them in order to
deprive them of the privilege which they had enjoyed
for a number of years in regard to the Muir.   This lawsuit is involved in mystery, and we suppose will ever
remain so; but we shall just endeavour to state the
facts as far as they can be made out from the badly
written papers connected with the process, and allow
our readers to pass their own judgment on the matter.
John Watson said in his application to the Court of
Session, that he purchased the estate of Dunnikier
just as it was, without any service or reservation to
any party whatever, and that consequently he was not
under any obligation to grant the feuars the privilege
in the Muir which they claimed.   The feuars, on the
other hand, defended their right, on the ground of the
original grant by Robert Lundie, sen., in 1608, above
referred to.

In the same year 1666, the Court granted a decreet
of reduction against the feuars ; but, notwithstanding,
considered it necessary that a certain portion of the
Muir should be set apart for their use in regard to their
building and repairing their houses, and appointed the
Laird of Collingtoun to go to Dunnikier and examine
the buildings, and also the Muir, and endeavour to decide how much of the Muir would be sufficient for the
feuars' purposes.   He went accordingly, and he stated
the number of houses then built to be 80 in number.
Yet what is very stange, he seemed to have supposed

that three acres of the Muir would be quite sufficient
for the use of the feuars, and that at some future time
they might get more if they required it. That was in
1668, but the case was in the hands of the Court until
1670, when they sent over six gentlemen, (the Laird
of Bogie being one of them,) to Dunnikier, to examine
and report, as the former commissioner's labours had
not decided the matter. These six gentlemen did not
decide the matter either, for they could not agree in
their opinion, and so they brought in no report, but
remitted the matter back to the Court, with a request
that one of the Lords of Session should be sent over to
Dunnikier along with them. Whether this request was
complied with or not we cannot say, but we find that
in November 1670, the feuars granted an obligation to
John Watson of 18 acres of the said Muir, and this
document was registered in the Regality Court Books
of Dunfermline, but not until April 25, 1684.

We have already said that a deep mystery hangs
over this lawsuit about the Muir, and also the resignation
of the 18 acres. It appears strange indeed that the Court
of Session should have granted a decreet against the
feuars ; thus to all intents and purposes depriving them
of the privilege which they had enjoyed for fifty-eight
years, and yet, at the same time, declaring it to be
necessary that a certain portion of the Muir should be
set apart for their use, and to be at the trouble of
sending first one gentleman over to Dunnikier to examine into the state of matters, and give his decision in
the case ; and when he entirely failed in his mission,
to send six *other* gentlemen to try their skill in bringing
the dispute to a successful issue. It would certainly
have been more consonant with the principles of strict
justice to have, in the first place, obtained the evidence

from properly qualified persons regarding the amount
of material which the feuars found it necessary to resort
to the Muir to obtain for the building and repairing
their houses, and then to have given a decreet agreeable to that evidence.   But as we have seen, the Court
acted very differently, and in consequence of their out of
the way proceedings, the lawsuit was protracted from
1666 to 1670, when it was settled, *not* by the Court
giving a final decreet, but by the feuars resigning into
the hands of the superior 18 acres of the Muir.

We have often heard it asserted that the feuars of
1740 gave this 18 acres of Muir in exchange for
18 ells of additional burying-ground, and great reflec-
tion has been cast upon their memory in consequence.
But the account which we have been enabled to give of
the matter shews that they had no hand in the transaction ; for the 18 acres were resigned by the feuars of
1670 into the hands of John Watson, sen.   Whether
that resignation had any connexion with the granting
of the first piece of burying-ground by John Watson
(36 ells), we cannot say.   And, moreover, as some
have alleged lately that the feuars of 1792 resigned
all claim to the 18 acres, we merely remark that in
the document which the feuars of that period adhibited
their names to, there is not the remotest reference to
the 18 acres : it merely refers to the *west* half of the
Muir.

This resignation of the 18 acres is a very curious
matter.   After having obtained a decreet at the very
commencement against the feuars, John Watson appears to have been quite satisfied with 18 acres, out of
about 85 or more acres of which the Muir originally
consisted, and then after this portion was put into his
hands, he did not register the deed until more than

thirteen years had elapsed, namely, in April 1684; and besides, three months after, namely, in July 1684, he gave to the feuars and other inhabitants the first piece of burying-ground. And we may just add here, that one grand reason why the whole affair is enveloped in mystery, is the circumstance, that, although the papers connected with the matter have been examined by skilful persons, no one has been able to read them. The only conclusion that we can come to regarding the matter is, that after a protracted lawsuit an amicable understanding was come to by the parties.

The feuars continued to take stones and clay, fail and divets from the Muir, as they required them, for the building and repairing their respective habitations, until about the year 1792, when serious disputes arose between them and James Townsend Oswald, the then proprietor of Dunnikier. Of the origin or nature of these disputes, we have now no satisfactory knowledge, but, at last, Mr Oswald proposed to the feuars that the Muir should be divided as near as possible into two equal parts, he keeping absolute possession of the west half to cultivate it, or make any use of it that he pleased, and the feuars having the same absolute right over the east half. This proposal was accepted by the feuars, and accordingly, on the 21st of May in the same year, they, to the number of eighty, signed a renunciation of their right of servitude over the west half of the Muir of Dunnikier in favour of Mr Oswald, he at the same time promising to give, by charter, to the feuars of Dunnikier, *alias* Pathhead, the absolute right of property in the east half. Accordingly, in fulfilment of this written promise, he granted a charter, March 29, 1793:—" To the members of the Burial Yard Box, [the only organised body existing in the

town at that time,] in name and for behoof of the
whole feuars in the said town of Dunnikier, and their
heirs and successors, being feuars in the said town, for
their respective rights and interests, heritably and ir-
redeemably, without any manner of redemption, rever-
sion, or regress, all and whole of the east half of the
Muir of Dunnikier, measuring thirty-three acres two
roods and thirty-six falls or thereby ; " on payment of
one penny Scots money at the term of Martinmas, if
asked only.

It must be noted here, however, that in terms of
this charter, Mr Oswald retained the right to all
metals and minerals below the surface of the ground
in the whole Muir, with the exception of freestone.
But here it must be added, that every individual
charter granted by the superiors of Dunnikier, since the
above amicable settlement of the differences between
James Townsend Oswald, Esq., and the feuars, contains the following clause :—" And I hereby give,
grant, and dispone, to the said ———, and foresaids,
a proportional right to the east half of the Muir of Dunnikier, *and other privileges* particularly specified in the
feu-charter granted by me to the feuars of Dunnikier
beforementioned." These privileges were—First, a
quarry near the Denburn bridge, on the farm of Smea-
town, without the payment of surface damage, which
has long been disused by the feuars, and of late years
has been entirely filled up. The reason of its being
abandoned was said to be the inadequacy of the drain
to carry off the water from it ; but although not generally known, yet it is a fact, that there is a capacious
and deep drain on the *south* side of the bridge, worked
towards the quarry, to the extent of thirteen yards,

which must bring it within a very few yards of the required distance. Why this work was abandoned in the early part of this century, after having been carried on so far, I have never learned. Second, the bleaching green at the same spot, commonly called "the Panney," and the springs on the east side of the burn commonly called "the Panney Well." Third, the right of quarrying stones in the sea-braes ; and Fourth, the right of quarrying on the rocks in the sands.

In 1796, the eastern half of the Muir, now the sole property of the feuars, was divided into six fields, properly fenced ; five of these were let to Mr James Nairn, Kirkcaldy, for nineteen years, but in 1804, he sublet the farm to Mr David Low, to which transaction the feuars gave their consent. In 1806, the south-east field, which had hitherto been allowed to lie in its natural state, for the purpose of supplying with divets, &c., those feuars who still required them, was also let to Mr Low. The whole rent that was drawn from the farm, from 1796 to 1814 inclusive, was £20, 8s. In the last-named year, it was let to Mr Alexander Robertson, for a period of nineteen years, at a rent of £100 ; from which sum, however, he obtained several deductions from time to time, but in 1826 he became bankrupt. The farm was then let to Mr Andrew Christie, for nineteen years, at an annual rent of £80, but deductions were made also to him on several occasions, and in 1833, the feuars agreed to make an annual deduction of £10 from the stipulated rent, thus reducing it to £70. On the expiry of Mr Christie's lease in 1845, the farm was let to Mr Andrew Pearson, for nineteen years, at an annual rent of £90. He died in 1859, but his heirs still retain possession. The tack expires at Martinmas 1864.   In 1837, a march wall was built on the west side of the farm, at the joint expense of Sir John Oswald and the feuars.

In the year 1813, Mr Brotherston, second minister of Dysart, applied to the Teind Court for an augmentation of stipend, and in this application he included a demand from the feuars, for stipend from their farm, for the years 1811, 1812, and 1813.   In the year 1791, the Government brought in a bill for the augmentation of stipends, but they found that the country gentlemen were too strong for them, and the bill was abandoned.   However, in 1810, an Act was passed for bringing all stipends up to £150 a-year.   But be it observed, that this augmentation was to be furnished by the Exchequer of Scotland ; and the ministers had still the privilege of demanding augmentations from the heritors, when teinds were not exhausted.   This was the first demand that had been made for teinds from the feuars' property.   Mr Brotherston, in due course, obtained his demands.   The feuars were adjudged to pay £      for the three years specified above ; and, besides, they had to pay a legal gentleman the sum of £14 or £15 for resisting the claim.

It was now supposed by everybody that the decision of the Teind Court on this occasion was a final settlement of the question, at least for the time being.   But this turned out to be an egregious mistake ; for about the year 1830, Mr David Murray, the *first* minister of Dysart, raised a process of augmentation before the Teind Court, which was not finally settled until the year 1835.   It then appeared that the settlement of the teinds in 1812 was merely an interim one, and that, by that settlement, some of the heritors had been paying too little, while some had been paying too much,

for the last twenty years.    Among the former were the
feuars of Pathhead.    Accordingly, in the spring of that
year, a demand was made upon them of £235, which
sum was to be given to those heritors who had been
paying too much.    However, one of the feuars, amusing
himself in looking over the figures in a large account of
the state of the teinds for the whole parish, consisting
of many pages, discovered an error of £30 in the add-
ing up of the feuars' account.    This was immediately
pointed out to Mr Mackenzie, the law-agent whom the
feuars had employed to defend them in the Court, and
who happened to be at the sea-bathing at Dysart at
the time.    That gentleman at once perceived that the
feuars had been charged with £30 more than their just
proportion.    The account was accordingly sent back to
Edinburgh, when the feuars' account was reduced by
£31; but there was a charge made of several pounds
for the feuars' proportion of making up the account,
which brought up the sum which they had to pay to
£210, 3s. 4d.

While on this point, it remains for us to notice the
demand which was made at the same time on the
feuars by Dundas and Wilson, the law-agents of the
Earl of Rosslyn in Edinburgh, for teinds, previous to
the year 1810, when Mr Brotherston made his first
claim.    These gentlemen calculated that the feuars
part of the Muir had been cultivated from the year
1793, when the charter was given; whereas it was
not let until 1796; and they calculated the rent, from
1793 until 1810, at the same value it was in 1830.
There is no document in existence now to prove the
amount of this new demand; but the impression on
our mind is, that it was £95.    We feel ourselves
under the necessity of explaining, for the sake of some

individuals, the meaning of this demand.   The Earl of
Rosslyn is what is called the titular of the teinds of
the parish of Dysart.   He has a legal right to the
teinds of any lands in the parish, previous to the time
when the minister of the parish applies for them.
This privilege has been in the family for a number of
generations.   The feuars considered this demand a
very unjust one, and they appointed the treasurer, and
another member of committee, to go to Edinburgh, and
wait on Dundas and Wilson, and endeavour to get the
demand reduced, or, if possible, set aside altogether.
They accordingly went to Edinburgh, taking with them
a carefully-prepared document, shewing what had been
the gross income of the farm previous to 1810, and
what the feuars had laid out upon it during the same
period.   The legal gentlemen saw at once that their
demand on the feuars could not be sustained; the clear
profit of the farm was so very trifling, that there was
next to nothing to levy teinds from; and they said that
they were quite willing of themselves to renounce the
claim for back teinds, on behoof of the Earl of Rosslyn,
but that they must write to his lordship and obtain his
sanction.   In a few days a letter came from Dundas
and Wilson, purporting that he had, according to their
advice, relinquished his claim on the feuars altogether,
but that the foresaid sum of £210, 3s. 4d. must be
paid to them *immediately* on behoof of *all* the heritors
who had been paying more than their legal proportion
of stipend for so many years back.   In a few days the
feuars paid the money.

Since the settlement of the teind question in 1835,
Pathhead Muir has paid of stipend to the first minister
of Dysart fully £11 annually, which is certainly a very

heavy ecclesiastical tax for a spot of little more than thirty acres of arable land.

The rent of this small farm is of immense importance to the inhabitants of this place; for, although it is very heavily burdened with poor-rates, income-tax, statute labour money, county assessment, and minister's stipend, it still has a clear profit of £50 to £60 annually. This money is wholly laid out in making improvements in streets and roads, &c., so that the public generally, and not the feuars alone, receive the benefit of it. The feuars have all the trouble of management, but no exclusive benefit. Had Pathhead Muir remained till now in the same state as it was in previous to 1793, it would not have been worth a single farthing to the feuars and other inhabitants, for no one now stands in need of clay and divets to build or repair houses with, the thatched roofs being now all but a matter of history. It was a happy idea which was acted upon in 1793, to divide and cultivate it. And, we may add, that a very great improvement has taken place in regard to it of late years, by draining, &c., at the mutual expense of the feuars and the tenant, so that it now bears remarkably good crops of every kind.

## EDUCATION.

In no respect has Scotland made more rapid strides towards perfection, during the present century, than in regard to education. We say *towards* perfection, for, although great progress has been made, we are not yet arrived at the summit. The town of Pathhead has fully kept pace with the other towns of Scotland in this respect, as it is now our privilege to note.

We have not been able to obtain the least glimpse of light about the state of education in this town and vicinity, until far down in the last century. Schools and teachers there must have been of some sort long previous to that period; but if we are to judge of their character by what we know did exist towards the end of the century, they must have been very far below the mark. In the beginning of the century there were some individuals in this place who could write well, but whether they were *sticket ministers*, or schoolmasters, or both, we cannot tell. In the latter half of the century, however, we have the names, and merely the names, of those individuals who then took upon them the arduous task of teaching the rising generation: Messrs Peter Smith, (who died in 1772,) Thomas Allen, David Fenton, Reid Menzies, Andrew Scott, and, we rather think, some others, down to the end of the century, were teachers in the town. We have ascertained nothing about either the intellectual or moral qualifications of these individuals, with the exception of Mr Menzies, who is said to have been a very effective teacher, pupils coming even from Kirkcaldy to attend his school. We have to record it to his honour, that he was the first teacher in this neighbourhood who set his face against the barbarous practice of cockfighting, which was then very general in other schools. He was a probationer of the Church of Scotland, and, after he left this place, he obtained a parish church in Orkney. There is one thing which we have remarked regarding individuals who received their education either in this town or elsewhere seventy years ago, or further back—that, although they might write a good firm hand, they were in many instances deplorably deficient in spelling. And, moreover, the great mass o

the daughters of working-men were incapable of sign-
ing their names to any document when necessary, but
substituted their mark instead; and this was the case,
or next to it, with many of the male sex.

There was one circumstance connected with education in this place, previous to the year 1794, which
had a most unfavourable effect upon the rising generation. We refer to the total want of a suitable school-
house. Owing to this unfortunate circumstance, the
inhabitants, however well qualified they might be to
judge what education ought to be, and however anxious
they might be to have their children well taught, had
no control whatever over the teachers. If they were
dissatisfied with his moral character or with his fitness
for teaching, all they could do in such a case was to
withdraw their children from his school, but they had
no other school to send them to in the town. So when
any individual came to the place, who imagined that
he was qualified to conduct a school, and rented a
house for that purpose, those who wished their children
taught to read the Bible and write a little, had no choice
but just to send them to the school, however ill qualified the teacher might happen to be. If there had been
a good school-house belonging to the inhabitants generally, or to any institution, and consequently a control
over the teachers, a decided improvement in the nature
of the education conferred on the rising generation
would have been the result.

It is very remarkable that we can at present point
out all the different places which were used as school-
houses during the latter half of last century, all standing in much the same condition as when so occupied.
There is one in Back Street, now used as a slaughter-
house, which was occupied, we believe, by two or three

teachers in succession ; another at the foot of Mitchel's
Wynd, west side ; another in Geekie's, now Law's
Close, occupied now as a weaver's shop and dwelling-
house ; another in Flesh Wynd, at present a grocer's
cellar ; and then, in the east end of Nether Street, two
doors west from the bridge, with an iron rail in front,
stands the kitchen school-room, where the worthy Mrs
Forgan for so many years taught boys and girls to read,
and the latter to knit and sew ; and next door west from
that, in the upper flat, west end, is the apartment in
which Mr Menzies, already referred to, kept school.
Let any one just take the trouble of inspecting these
quondam school-houses, and he will heartily agree with
us in saying that the school accommodation in this
place in the olden time was scanty and wretched in the
extreme, crippling the energies of the teachers, and
highly injurious in more respects than one to the
scholars.

But the inhabitants of Pathhead, about the year
1794, being fully aware of the very unfavourable position in which their children were placed, in not having
a comfortable school-room within their reach where
they might be taught by an efficient teacher, felt the
necessity of doing what was in their power to remedy
the evil. They, in short, resolved that they would
build a school-house. But we will give their views in
their own words :—

" The flourishing and populous town of Pathhead,
finding their town greatly increase, both in its inhabitants and sources of trade ; but they found that they
had laboured under a great disadvantage for the instruction of youths, and they had no stated means of education for generations back. Therefore, that the inhabitants of this flourishing place might have the satisfac-

tion of having their children instructed in every useful branch of education, without being obliged to send them to distant schools, they met at large, and agreed that a school-house was not only necessary to be had among them, but agreed that one should be built as soon as possible, and that the expense should be raised by a general subscription among the inhabitants, and any donations wherewith they might be favoured."

This was the preamble, and then follows the subscribers' names. We shall just add the minute of the first public meeting :—

" *Pathhead Meeting-House, Jan.* 28, 1794. — In consequence of an advertisement, per the town officer, a number of the subscribers for the laudable purpose of building a school-house being met, time and place as above, made choice of James Bogie for preses ; then proceeded to make choice of a committee of their number to conduct the business in their absence, and to do and act therein as they shall see cause, when the following persons were unanimously chosen for said purpose, viz.—David Millie, jun., John Bennet, Walter Greig, David Davidson, Alex. Ingram, James Penman, Roger Black, John Goodsir, and James Bogie, treasurer. At same time made choice of the following persons to collect or gather in the cash, viz.—Henry Philp and George Oswald, Back Street ; David Young and James Thomson, Mid Street ; William Ramsay and James Walker, Nether Street ; John Tod and Henry Rait, jun., St Clairtown."

These individuals, thus authorised, set themselves zealously to work to secure funds for the erection of the proposed school-house. Contracts were entered into, and the long desiderated building was erected, 27 feet by 18 within—the school-room on the ground-flat with dwelling-house for the teacher above. Mr David Sheck was appointed as the first teacher.

But notwithstanding all the apparent anxiety on the part of the inhabitants generally to have a school-house erected, yet when the money came to be collected, the zeal of many had cooled down, and even several who had put down their names in the subscription list drew back, and the committee was under the necessity of prosecuting some of those individuals for their subscriptions. It appeared then, as it has often done since, that there is a very great difference between holding up the hand at a public meeting and putting it into the pocket and bringing something out. The assistance given by wealthy individuals *outside* the district was quite trifling, and *in* the district, while some gave respectably in proportion to their means, others gave little, while a number, who could have given a little, gave nothing. It consists with the writer's personal knowledge that there were a number of individuals in the place who could have given something towards the object, and some even liberally, who never countenanced it in the least. If all these had given according to their means, the work would have been easy and pleasant. But there are three circumstances which ought to be taken into consideration in accounting for the keeping back so many from contributing. First, there was the absolute poverty of many. Wages were very low, in particular the nailers, who were still numerous in the district at that time. Second, there would be, no doubt, a considerable number who were quite content to let things just remain as they were, and as they had been in their fathers' and grandfathers' time. There is no doubt that they, in common with the rest of the inhabitants of Scotland, wished their children to be educated; but this wish included little more than a capability of reading the Bible. If the boys could read that sacred Book without stopping, and could write a little, they were considered well educated, and fit to go to a trade. But the girls were worse off still, for very few of them were taught to write, as we have already noticed. They were quite satisfied with this system, without making any exertion to bring about a better state of things. The third circumstance was, that the time of giving away money for the support of objects beyond one's own family was not yet arrived— the age of benevolence had not commenced. The first missionary society that was established in Great Britain, and which has been the honoured instrument of doing a great amount of good in the world, was formed in a back parlour a few months before the people of Pathhead began to build their school-house : the total amount of the parlour subscription was £13, 12s. 6d. And there were no Heriots nor Watsons come to our side of the water, no Philps had yet risen up to aid the people of Pathhead in raising their first educational edifice. They had to struggle alone (those who engaged in the work) and with all the difficulties, too, which generally attend a first attempt to attain a praiseworthy object. Never, I believe, was a committee more harassed and worried in prosecuting their labours than the committee of the first subscription school in Pathhead. The house had been built as projected, the tradesmen's bills had to be paid, but a sufficient sum of money to meet the demands on the committee was not forthcoming, and money had to be borrowed from three benefit societies in the town, on bills bearing interest.

But instead of the circumstances of the subscribers

growing better as time rolled on, they became worse.
The interest of the debt was running on ; in some instances, the bills were renewed by the committee, but
they had no funds out of which they could even pay
the interest, far less to reduce the principal. A second
subscription among the inhabitants was attempted, but
it yielded very little. Various other schemes were
proposed for raising more money, but were equally un-
profitable. Meantime, some of the creditors became
very clamorous for their money, and one bill was pro-
tested. In short, during the eight years that the subscribers' committee had the school-house under their
management, its office was anything but pleasant. At
the end of that period they were effectually relieved.
We shall now proceed to state how, and in what manner, the committee was delivered from its unpleasant
position.

One of the plans which were proposed by the subscribers at their meetings, was to petition the feuars
of Pathhead and St Clairtown to take the property off
their hands altogether, and pay the debt which had
been incurred—(which, it would appear, had mounted
up to about £50)—the feuars, of course, to keep it up
as a public school, for the benefit of the inhabitants of
Pathhead and St Clairtown. A petition to that effect
was sent in November 1801, but it was rejected by
both bodies of feuars. However, not very long after
this—namely, on 12th August 1802—an agreement
was come to between the school subscribers and the
feuars of Pathhead ; the latter accepting of the school-
house, with all the debt, and also taking upon them the
whole responsibility of keeping it up as a public school
for the benefit of the inhabitants of the district. By
this agreement the subscribers were relieved from a

burden which they were not able to bear. It was a very providential circumstance that the feuars by that time were in a position to relieve them. Had the difficulties of the subscribers occurred six or seven years sooner, it would have been altogether out of the power of the feuars to have interposed between them and irretrievable ruin—that is to say, as an educational body. They would have been under the necessity of selling the property, and, in consequence, the progress of education would have been arrested for an indefinite period of time. The object of the subscribers was evidently twofold—first, to erect an edifice, in a convenient and healthy situation, where the pupils might receive a sound and useful education; and, second, that this edifice might be reared free from debt. In the first they succeeded; in the second they failed. But another party was providentially raised up to secure the second also.

Some may be of opinion that we have dwelt longer on this part of the subject than its importance warrants—that the subscribers to the school did not deserve much gratitude for all that they accomplished in regard to education. We merely say, in reply, that we are of a different opinion. In estimating the progress which individuals or communities make, we must not only take notice of the elevation which they reach, but also the platform from which they arise; and their platform was surely low enough. The subscribers' work was a *first* attempt; and, like all other *first* attempts to achieve anything of importance, it was beset with discouraging circumstances; and we conceive that they deserve the gratitude of posterity for giving the cause of education a local habitation and a name in the town of Pathhead.

It does not appear that the first four or five teachers of this school were individuals in *all* respects qualified for their vocation. When the first one left to be parish schoolmaster of Burntisland, there was, indeed, much regret expressed on both sides; but there was one teacher to whom the subscribers *gave liberty* to go away; and there was another whom the feuars, shortly after they had taken possession of the premises, *sent away*.

The feuars had but a sorry bargain of the school-house. Its construction was faulty in several respects; and it thus cost them a good deal of money in improving and repairing it during the forty seven years it was in their possession.

But it is now our pleasant task to record another step of progress in regard to education in the town of Pathhead. In July 1816, Mr Campbell, who had been teaching in the town school for some time, sent in his resignation to the feuars. There were, of course, several meetings of the committee, and also several general meetings of the feuars held, for the purpose of appointing another teacher. There were two candidates who offered themselves to fill the vacancy. One of the candidates was Mr George Johnson, from Burntisland, with good certificates; the other was Mr William Todd, who had commenced his teaching in Gallatown, afterwards he had a school in Birrel Street, and, at the time he offered himself, he was teaching in a house which stood precisely where the west side of Nairn's factory now stands. There is a certain degree of obscurity in the minutes of the feuars in regard to this matter; but the real fact was, some favoured the one candidate, and some favoured the other. It, however, occurred to some individuals that there was a sufficient number of chil-

dren in the town to fill *two* schools; and, therefore, it
was proposed to give Mr Johnson the town school,
and allow Mr Todd an annual sum equal to the valued
rent of the town school. This proposition met with
general approbation, and two tradesmen were appointed
to value the school accordingly. The value they set
upon school-room and dwelling-house was £9. This
valuation was ratified by the feuars; and, accordingly,
this sum was paid annually to Mr Todd, and its cur-
rency commenced the day that Mr Johnson began to
teach. Certain regulations were agreed on by the
feuars for the guidance of the teachers : they were to
be placed exactly upon a level. One item we may
mention—namely, that each teacher was to teach, *gratis*,
four children, who were to be selected by the committee
of feuars. Thus two schools were now established in
the town, and the school-rooms rent free to the teachers,
whereas formerly there was none. This, we repeat,
was another important step in the right direction.

But the most important step in the progress of education that had yet taken place in Pathhead is that
which it is now incumbent on us to record; namely,
the establishment of Philp's Institution. The setting
up of this institution in our midst put all former attempts to educate the rising generation entirely in the
shade. Here was both the will and the power to do good
combined. Robert Philp, Esq., of Edenshead, during
his long pilgrimage, clearly saw the existence of a
great evil in the neighbourhood where he lived, and
also the cause of it; namely, a want of education,
arising from the poverty or carelessness of parents,
and he determined that he would apply a remedy, as
far as his means would allow him. On the 15th of
May 1820, he executed a deed, conveying to trustees

named by him, *his whole property*, heritable and movable, (with the exception of a few legacies,) for the purpose of affording education in the different districts he mentions, " to that class of children who, from the poverty of their parents, were most likely to be deprived of that blessing—the most needy to have the first claim." In carrying out this resolution, he appointed " the laying out two-eighths of the whole free rent or interest of his property in educating the class above mentioned in Kirkcaldy ; three-eighths in the same manner, and for the same purpose, in Pathhead, St Clairtown, and Hawkleymuir ; two-eighths in Linktown, Newtown of Abbotshall, and Inverteil ; and one-eighth in Kinghorn ; and that the children at all the schools should be taught to read English, writing, and arithmetic, and should be furnished from the funds with books, paper, pens, ink, and slates ; and that, moreover, their religious instruction should be attended to, as being of the greatest importance to reasonable creatures ;" hence he enjoins that " they should be taught the doctrines and principles of the Christian religion, as these are contained in the Scriptures, in an easy, plain, and familiar manner, and the teachers giving them select passages to commit to memory ;" and as he very justly observes, " this will enable them to understand the religion of Jesus Christ, and must, through the divine blessing, have a very favourable influence on their minds and character."

Moreover, Mr Philp says, " that as Sabbath evening schools had been found by experience to conduce very considerably to the improvement of children, as well as of those who are further advanced in years, he appoints and directs a Sabbath evening school to be kept in each of the four districts named above, and

directing that the teachers of said schools shall receive
remuneration according to circumstances, and also,
that coal, candle, books, &c., be furnished for said
schools out of the funds. And that further, in addition,
the scholars shall be taught sacred music. And further,
if the funds would afford it, he directs that the scholars
shall receive annually, clothing to the amount of thirty
shillings, and also, when they leave school, they
shall receive a sum of money." And in order to carry
out these provisions, certain individuals residing in
Kirkcaldy were to be appointed to act along with the
trustees as governors and managers ; but that in order
to lighten the labours of these persons, local managers
were to be appointed in each of the other three districts. In Pathhead six managers were to be chosen
occupying houses of seven pounds rent, and four from
St Clairtown, occupying houses of five pounds rent ;
but the whole ten individuals to act together as a body
of managers for the district of Pathhead, St Clairtown,
and Hawkleymuir. The election of the governors and
managers in Kirkcaldy, and also the local managers in
all the other three districts, to take place every two
years.

Mr Philp died on the 14th April 1828, but it took
the governors and managers a considerable time to
make arrangements for carrying out fully the objects
of the trust, and consequently the local managers for
Pathhead, &c., were not chosen until January 25,
1830. On the 29th March following, the local managers made choice of 150 scholars, and sent 50 of
them to Mr Johnson, 50 to Mr Todd, and 50 to Mr
Boyd, who, at that time, taught a school in Hawkleymuir. This, however, was only a temporary measure, as the local managers were determined on building

a. sufficiently capacious school-house to hold the whole
number, or more, if required at any future period.
Accordingly, the splendid edifice in Nether Street was
erected, with every necessary convenience connected
with it. The main school-room occupies the whole
area of the building, and is on a level with the street,
while below, there are two school-rooms, a larger and
a smaller, both well lighted. All these school-rooms
are occupied, as we shall shew presently. Mr Todd
was appointed sole teacher on 23d September 1831,
and the school was formally opened February 6, 1832.

The local managers of Pathhead from the first considered that it would be a very wise and economical
plan to establish a female school in connexion with the
institution, as by this means they would get all the
frocks and shirts and stockings, &c., for the scholars
made under their own eye, while, at the same time,
the girls would be taught sewing and knitting. This
plan has been carried out until the present time, and
is found to work well.

Agreeably to the provisions of Mr Philp's will, a
Sabbath evening school was established, at the very
commencement of the institution, in this place; and
the local managers have always kindly permitted children to attend this school who do not belong to the
weekly school, and a goodly number avail themselves
of the privilege.

There is a very interesting circumstance connected
with Mr Philp's property, so generously devoted to the
education of the poor. The trustees, after careful
examination of his affairs, found, to their no small
gratification, that a very large increase in the value of
his property had taken place in the interval between
the executing of the will and his death, a period of

about eight years, and they found themselves under the
necessity of acting, in some respects, a little different
from the letter of the will, although, as they thought,
quite agreeable to its spirit. They wished for a remedy
for this state of things. The only plan which they
could devise, was to endeavour to obtain an Act of
Parliament, which would warrant them to carry out
the benevolent design of the donor to its fullest extent.
The governors and managers accordingly applied for
and obtained the proposed Act, it receiving the royal
assent, August 3, 1846. In various respects this Act
of Parliament was virtually an Act of indemnity to the
governors and managers for their past conduct, for they
had entered into various arrangements which were not
provided for in the trust-deed, such as investing money
in landed property, building school-houses, establishing
female schools for sewing and knitting, &c. But farther
alterations were made ; such as constituting the governors and managers a corporate body, under the title of
" The Governors of Robert Philp's Trust-Estate and
Schools." Other clauses were introduced into the Act,
but we shall only mention one, which we conceive to
be of very great importance to the class for whose
benefit Mr Philp's property was intended ; namely, the
power conferred on the various district-managers
to admit additional scholars to the schools. This
power these managers have availed themselves of,
so that in Pathhead school, since the passing of
the Act, there has been, instead of 150, as the
trust-deed authorises, from 250 to 300 scholars
attending, just according to the extent of the funds.

These schools have now been in operation during a
period of thirty-two years, and every one who knows

anything of the matter will allow that they have been
immense blessings to a very great number of individuals.
There have been hundreds of children who have obtained
a good education in Philp's Institution, who would never
otherwise have got any education worth mentioning.
The second generation, in many instances, are now attending the school in Pathhead, and numbers of the
first scholars have been fitted for, and are now filling,
places of trust, for which they would not, in all proba-
bility, have been fitted otherwise. Besides, the clothing
which they receive from year to year is a very great
benefit to the children belonging to poor families. But
there is another circumstance which ought by no means
to be overlooked in estimating the advantages which
children derive from this institution, namely, their
coming so much into contact with the Word of God.
The lessons which they are taught have all a moral and
religious bearing ; and especially the Sabbath evening
school is *exclusively* devoted to religious instruction.
The benefits which pupils derive from Philp's Institution will not be exhausted by time, but will most certainly reach forward into eternity.

We now return to the "Old Town School," as we
shall now denominate the "Subscription School" of
1794. In the year 1835 Mr Johnson left, and Mr
Andrew Wilson, teacher in Buckhaven, was appointed
to succeed him. It deserves to be mentioned here that
the feuars were so very anxious to obtain a teacher who
would give satisfaction to the *whole* community, that
they called a meeting of the inhabitants for the purpose
of giving their assistance and advice in the matter.
The inhabitants met accordingly in the Town Hall, and,
as already stated, Mr Wilson was ultimately the object
of their choice. There was another circumstance con-

nected with the appointment of Mr Wilson which deserves to be noticed.    Instead of advertising for a teacher, as is generally the case when a vacancy occurs, they appointed three individuals to go and visit several schools which were within their reach, without giving any warning to the respective teachers, and see the manner in which these schools were conducted and the progress which the pupils had made, and come back and make a report to a future meeting.    This plan was carried out, and the members of the deputation were unanimous in their report in recommending Mr Wilson as the best qualified individual to fill the vacancy.    Mr Wilson was accordingly appointed unanimously at the second meeting of the inhabitants.    But it further deserves to be remarked, that Mr Wilson expressly stipulated that his coming to Pathhead depended on certain improvements being made in the school-room, in order to make it more suitable for teaching upon the newest and most approved system.    The feuars consented to the carrying out of these improvements, on the understanding that the inhabitants generally should be called upon to contribute towards the expense.    The proposed improvements were accordingly made at an expense, we believe, of about £40, the feuars giving £3.    The inside stair was removed and a stone stair erected outside, thus enlarging the school-room considerably ; a porch was built outside the door, making the place more comfortable ; the old fixed seats were removed and movable forms substituted ; tables and seats were placed round the walls for the convenience of the writing classes, and the whole area of the school-room made available for teaching.    Besides, the stone pavement was removed and a wooden floor laid down, which was lowered a foot below the old level.    Mr Wilson

C

accordingly came, and commenced teaching; but it was not long before he found the school-room still too small, and was under the necessity of sending a class to the Town Hall to be taught by an assistant.

This system went on for a few years, but a dissatisfaction with the old school-room began to lodge in the minds of many of the most respectable and judicious of the inhabitants of the locality. The *house* itself had been decidedly improved; it had been somewhat enlarged and made more convenient, but still it was considered to be far below what the educational wants of the community required in various respects. When it was built in 1794, it had not a rival in the whole parish of Dysart, and at that time it had a free circulation of pure air around it; but in 1848 it was closed in with houses and garden walls, &c., that had been erected, and thus it was justly considered as being in a great measure unfit for congregating together such a large number of children as then came to be taught, notwithstanding of 150 being drawn off to Philp's Institution. Besides, it was so very inferior to the splendid building that had been erected in Nether Street by Philp's Managers, that those who at one time looked upon it as a very grand and suitable structure had now fairly lost all conceit of it; in short, it was now considered indispensable that a new school-house and dwelling-house should be built.

There was one favourable circumstance connected with this movement, however. The British Government had been in the practice for some time previous of giving grants of money to assist in the erection of school-houses and dwelling-houses for the teachers in certain circumstances and on certain conditions. Application was accordingly made by the subscribers to the proposed new school for a share of the fund at the disposal of the Government Council of Education. The reply was decidedly favourable; but, as we have said, these Government grants were only given on certain conditions, and the strict fulfilment of these conditions was in every case indispensable to receiving the money. Consequently a long correspondence took place between the subscribers and the Council of Education; and at last, when the schoolhouse, with dwelling-house attached, had been erected, the subscribers obtained the grant of £293 from the Commissioners. Besides, it was understood by the subscribers from the very first, that the feuars were willing to sell the old town school-house, and give the proceeds (say £100) as a donation to assist in building the new one. The old edifice was accordingly sold by public auction on May 11, 1849, and the £100 paid over to the Committee of the Pathhead and St Clairtown Subscription School, as the new school was denominated, although the sum which the feuars received for their property fell short of that, after all expenses were paid. The feuars also delivered over to said committee, for the use of the school, a pair of globes, which had been presented to the old school by Bailie Walker in September 1837, also a table, chair, bookcase, &c.

But notwithstanding all the exertions which were made by the School Committee to obtain subscriptions, the funds fell short of meeting the expense of the erection. In these circumstances, the committee applied to the feuars on several occasions for assistance. Altogether, the feuars voted £35 in answer to these calls. But, over and above, in March 1858, the School Committee made application to the feuars for a sum of money to enable the subscribers to take advantage of an offer of £50 from Ferguson's Trustees, upon the condition of raising £100 by subscription——the whole sum of £150 to be laid out on good security as an endowment, the *interest only* to be available as ordinary income for the current expenses of the school. Agreeably to this request, the feuars voted a donation of £25 towards the object, on the condition that the school was to remain *undenominational*.

The Pathhead and St Clairtown Subscription School-house is very roomy and commodious; is well lighted, and occupies a very healthy position at the back of the railway. There has been a new class-room added, and some other improvements made lately, at a cost of £191, raised by subscription. There is a female teacher connected with the institution for teaching the girls sewing and knitting, as also four pupil-teachers who receive salaries from Government. The attendance of scholars is about 200.

The Old Town School is still occupied as a school-room; the attendance is not large.

We may also mention here, that a very commodious school-house was erected in Hawkleymuir without any Government grant, and opened in 1849: average attendance of scholars about 120. Also in Gallatown a very excellent school-house, with dwelling-house attached, was erected in 1861, assisted by Government, and opened in 1861.

Further, in the town of Dysart, in the year 1813, a very convenient and commodious Burgh School was built in an excellent situation. There is a good attendance of scholars. Also, in 1839, a very suitable Subscription School was built there, and has also a good attendance. There are several female schools in St Clairtown, Gallatown, and Dysart.

The vast superiority of the school accommodation in the present day, over that which existed in the last century, may well strike us with astonishment. The liberality which has been displayed by many individuals in this neighbourhood, who have again and again given of their substance for promoting the cause of education in this district, and even in the whole parish, is beyond all praise. Such liberality was never thought of by our forefathers. And, as we hinted at the beginning of this section, the superiority of school accommodation has an intimate connexion with superiority of teaching. The progress, in regard to the nature of the teaching, has kept pace with the progress which has been made in school-house building. It is a thorough education which children receive now. They are taught to understand their lessons, which was not the case formerly. The spelling now is perfect. All this implies that the teachers are better qualified now than they were seventy or eighty years ago. In whatever way we look at education now, we cannot help perceiving that we have made astonishing progress.

We cannot conclude our remarks on education without distinctly noticing the Sabbath evening schools which have sprung up in this quarter of late years. When the first school-house was built in Pathhead in 1794, we question very much if there was a single Sabbath evening school in Scotland—at least we are certain that there was none in this neighbourhood. But in the last five or six years of the eighteenth century, the inhabitants of this country began to awake as from sleep. A new light had begun to dawn upon them : they began to see that we must not only *pray* for the conversion of the heathen abroad, and the heathen at home, but that we must *work* as well as pray. They had seen with dismay a neighbouring nation violently tossed from the one extreme of soul-destroying and pauperising superstition to the opposite extreme of cheerless infidelity, all through ignorance of the Word of God. They began to send missionaries abroad, and at the same time to spread the knowledge of the Bible in our own country. And as it is the wisest plan, in regard to any enterprise, to begin at the beginning, Sabbath-school societies were organised in every part of the country for the purpose of imbuing the minds of the rising generation with divine truth. When this process was going on in other parts of the country, there was no necessity for a new organisation of this nature in Pathhead, for there was one already in existence here,—we allude to the committee of the school which had been recently erected. However, it is but doing justice to Mr David Sheck, the first teacher in that school, to state that he commenced the Sabbath evening school, *on his own* responsibility, on the last Sabbath of December 1797, in consequence of finding that it was almost entirely out of his power to communicate religious instruction to his scholars through the week, as they were getting so numerous. The numbers who came to the Sabbath evening school, both of old and young, actually filled the school-room ; and he called a meeting of the committee to solicit their aid and support. The committee readily responded to his call, and cheerfully aided him in conducting the school. It succeeded well for a year or two, but at last it fell off; but when Messrs Johnson and Todd were appointed as teachers in the town, they each of them bound themselves to teach a Sabbath evening school. Shortly after this, a Sabbath-School Society was formed in the parish of Dysart, and schools were accordingly set up in every part of it. The society almost died away, but was re-organised some years after; but the schools did not succeed so well as they ought to have done. And we may here just state, that from about the year 1824 to 1830, there was no Sabbath-school teacher in the town of Pathhead, excepting the writer. But, with thankfulness, we have to record the happy change that has taken place since the last-mentioned year. The societies here and elsewhere, we believe, have died out; but, what is found to be far better, schools of this description are managed and supported by the respective congregations in the locality. Every congregation in this neighbourhood has a large school and a Bible-class. Philp's Institution has a large one besides, as we have already noticed. There are, besides, Sabbath-schools in Hawkleymuir, Gallatown, &c., taught by the weekly teachers, and supported by the managers of the weekly schools.

## ECCLESIASTICALS.

Previous to the year 1747, there was only one solitary place of worship in the whole parish of Dysart—namely, the parish church, a portion of which is still standing, attached to the steeple. This place of worship was very small and inconvenient, was not fully seated, and was, besides, sadly out of repair, before the new church was built. But, in the above-mentioned year, the Seceders from the Church of Scotland having divided into two bodies—Burgher and Antiburgher—the congregation worshipping in the Links

kirk (as the Pathhead folks used to term it) split;
like many other congregations, one side espousing the
Burgher view of matters, and the other the Anti-
burgher. The latter party left, and fitted up an old
barn as a place of worship for themselves, near the
foot of the Old Path, being, as we understand, a few
yards east, or north-east, from the dwelling-house now
occupied by Mr Thomas Hutchison. This was probably the malting barn that was in existence there as
far back as the year 1595. This place of worship was
no doubt of a very homely character, such as the people
were able to obtain at the time. The ground at the
back of it was quite high, and people could sit on this
high ground, it has been said, and put their feet on
the roof. The congregation, however, continued to
meet in this house until an idea entered into the minds
of some individuals, one Sabbath, that the high ground
was pressing harder upon the walls than it had formerly
done, and a panic was the consequence, and the whole
of the people who happened to be present, rushed out,
and they never occupied it afterwards. One individual
whom we knew quite well, was so much alarmed, that
he jumped from the front of the gallery to the ground.
It may be proper to remark here, however, that the
individual referred to, was rather eccentric and impul-
sive, as the following anecdote will shew. One day
his better half was making broth, and she took a ladle-
ful out of the pot, and put it into a basin and gave it
to him. He sat down, and took the basin on his knee,
Scotch fashion, and began to partake, but finding the
morsel too hot, he cried out to his wife, " I ken what
ye mean noo ; ye mean to plot me to death," and then
instantly threw the basin and its contents under the
grate.

The congregation not having another house to go to, were under the necessity of meeting in the burying ground for worship, and did so for one whole winter at least; but Mr Thomson, their then minister, having purchased from Mr Oswald of Dunnikier, the house, with garden attached, now in the possession of his youngest son, Mr John Thomson, in the year 1763, granted a lease of a spot in the north part of the garden, for 247 years, at £6 Scots of rent, to the congregation, where they erected the present chapel. About the year 1803, a considerable addition was made to the height of the walls, new windows were put in, and the present substantial slate roof put on. A number of years afterwards, the original gallery was removed, and the present one erected. Subsequently, the old unsightly piece of Dunnikier garden wall, which stood at the front of the chapel, was removed, and a parapet wall, surmounted by an iron rail, erected in its room ; and further, in the beginning of this year, *all* the old seats were taken away, and replaced with new ones. Thus, although *the outside* of this place of worship may not please the taste of *every* passer by, yet, what is of far more consequence, *the inside* has been, first or last, entirely renovated, modernised, and beautified, and at the same time made more convenient and comfortable for the worshippers than it ever was before. Sittings formerly 795, but since the late improvements have been made, supposed to be somewhat fewer.

This congregation, as we have said, had its origin in the split of the Secession in 1747, but it was sometime in 1748 before they obtained a minister. Mr David Wilson was their first choice, but they were not long favoured with his services, for in 1752 he was called away to London, where he remained till his death, which took place in June 1784. He was a man of considerable abilities, and wrote several works, especially one named " Palemon's Creed Reviewed." We may here state, for the benefit of some of our readers, that " Palemon " was Robert Sandeman, son-in-law of John Glass, founder of the Glassites. Mr Wilson's successor at the foot of the Path was Mr Kay, but he left in 1757 ; what came of him we have not been able to ascertain. In November that year, Mr Thomas Thomson was ordained, and remained with the congregation until his death in —— 1789. He was succeeded in the pastorate by his son, Mr James Thomson, who died in —— 1801. Mr Thomas Gray was the next minister, but he died very suddenly in the session-house at noon on Sabbath —— 1837. Mr James Black then succeeded to the office, and still continues.

It may be proper to remark here, however, that when, in 1820, the Burghers and Anti-burghers reunited after a separation of seventy-three years, this congregation did not, *as a body,* favour this union. A considerable number of the members, however, warmly espoused it, and went off and built a chapel for themselves, at the east end of Kirkcaldy, joining themselves to the new body, which took to itself the name of " The United Secession Church." The remanent members of the Pathhead congregation, along with several other Anti-burgher congregations, who did not favour the above union, soon after joined in fellowship with several other congregations who had been for some time connected with the late Dr M'Crie, and this new organised body took to itself the title of Original Seceders. Further, in 1852, *the whole* of the congregations belonging to this body joined the Free Church of

Scotland. The place of worship in Pathhead which we have now been describing, goes by the name of "Dunnikier Free Church."

As we remarked in our Prefatory Notice, there are several portions of this narrative which must necessarily have a reference to St Clairtown, as well as Pathhead. The simple reason is, that the interests of the two districts, in regard to the points to which we refer, are identical. This was the case with our section on Education, and so here; yea, in the present section, it will even be necessary to include the town of Dysart.

In accordance with the foregoing remark, we have now to record the erection of the Relief Church in Dysart, a great number of its members belonging to Pathhead. This took place in 177–, shortly after the rise of the Relief body. But from what cause we know not, the congregation in Dysart did not obtain a minister until 1779, when Mr William Campbell was ordained. For several years after this century was begun, there was to be seen above the pulpit, the letters and figures as follows:— $\begin{smallmatrix} W \\ 17 \end{smallmatrix} \quad \begin{smallmatrix} C \\ 74 \end{smallmatrix}$ Mr Campbell died in 1792, and was succeeded by Mr William Billerwell, who died in ——. Mr Spence succeeded him, but he left in 1827. Mr William Adair Pettigrew was then ordained, but as he has become very infirm of late years, Mr Houston was ordained in November last, as his helper and successor. We are given to understand, however, that since Mr Houston's ordination, Mr Pettigrew has retired from active service altogether.

In the year 1842, this congregation, with all the rest of the congregations belonging to the Relief body, joined the United Secession Synod, and the two bodies thus joined together henceforth assumed the title of the

United Presbyterian Church.　The chapel in Dysart contains 750 sittings.

In the year 1802, the present parish church of Dysart was built.　It is very plain, but substantial and comfortable.　It presents a very striking contrast to the old parish church, which was built in Popish times, and was never fitted up in modern style, as a Protestant place of worship.　On October 20, 1816, a circumstance occurred in the new church, which was very near being attended with fatal consequences.　Mr George Muirhead, first minister of the parish, having accepted a call to the parish of Cramond, on the above named day intended to have preached his farewell sermon.　There was a very general turning out of the parishioners in consequence, and the church was crowded, when, as the service was just about commencing, an alarm was given that a part of the gallery was giving way.　A great uproar ensued, and the people rushing out in great confusion, a number of them got their clothes torn, but it fortunately happened that no one was seriously hurt after all.　Mr Muirhead afterwards published the sermon which he intended to have preached, and distributed it gratis among the members of the congregation.　Sittings 1600.

In the latter part of the last century, and during the first twenty years of the present one, it was a very interesting sight to behold the great numbers of people belonging to Pathhead going to and returning from the two places of worship in Dysart; namely, the Established Church and the Relief, on a Sabbath day. The old Dysart road being so straight and level, as we have noticed in another section, they might be seen filling the road nearly from the one end to the other; the young and robust getting in the front ranks, while

the feeble and aged among them were falling gradually
into the rear. This picturesque view has vanished.
The number of persons belonging to the formerly Relief congregation has fallen off considerably of late
years, but, as a young and active minister has been
settled among them, it is to be expected that in a short
time the chapel may again be filled, as it was fifty
years ago. But we now proceed to give the *principal*
reason for the falling off of the Sabbath traffic between
Pathhead and Dysart.

About the year 1821, the late Mr Peter Brotherston,
at that time first minister of Dysart, fitted up, in a
very neat and convenient manner, the school-room
occupied by Mr Todd in the Nether Street of Pathhead,
as a place of worship, and occupied it, or caused it to
be occupied as such, on Sabbath evenings. The suc-
cess of this experiment being equal to his expectations,
he proposed to several of the most wealthy of the ad
herents of the Established Church living in Pathhead
and St Clairtown, that they should combine in a kind
of joint-stock company and build a chapel ; promising
that if they did so, he would personally, or by proxy,
supply them with preaching, and they of course were
to get the seat-rents as interest for their money laid
out, but the door collections were to be handed over
to the Dysart Kirk-session for behoof of the poor. In
pursuance of this proposition, a small joint-stock company was formed, and the foundation-stone of a chapel
was laid in May 1822, and it was in due course opened.
It cost about £3000. The ministers of Dysart preached
alternately in it, and a good attendance was given to
the services. But in course of time, the congregation
came to be of opinion that it would be much better for
them to obtain a stated minister of their own ; and

accordingly, in the year 1840, they gave a call to Mr
Charles Jamieson to become their pastor, which he
accepted, and was settled among them.  But it turned
out, that at the time the chapel had been opened, the
proprietors had never received sufficient interest for
their money laid out in its erection.  This led to a
wish on their part to sell the chapel to the congregation.  The latter responded to this wish, and a general
and very liberal subscription was made by the members.
They also obtained assistance from various quarters,
and a bargain was finally struck between the parties;
the congregation giving the proprietors £1000 for the
chapel ; the latter thus actually incurring a loss of
£2000.  The Disruption of the Church of Scotland
took place not long after.  As the chapel was originally
built with the sanction of the Presbytery of Kirkcaldy,
and still continued under its superintendence after its
transfer, the congregation, who, almost to a man, with
Mr Jamieson at their head, joined the Free Church,
was deprived of all right and title to it.  It was so far
fortunate for the original proprietors, that they received
the £1000 *before* the Disruption took place, for if it
had occurred a little sooner, they would have received
nothing for their outlay of £3000.

The congregation were thus necessitated to begin
anew and build another chapel for themselves, at the
cost of about £1000.  It was opened in 1844.  But
as this place of worship, like many others belonging to
the Free Church, was very low in the walls, and had
likewise other defects, in the year 1859 a large sum of
money was subscribed by the congregation for the purpose of improving it, and, although sorely thwarted by
adverse circumstances, they succeeded at last in raising the walls to a sufficient height, with windows to

correspond, putting a complete gallery round it, a very neat belfry on the top of the west gable, and altogether giving it a very respectable appearance on the outside, and making it neat and commodious within. These improvements were made at a cost of £1250. This place of worship is denominated "Pathhead Free Church." Sittings 900.

And what became of the old chapel? posterity will ask. We simply answer, that although it may be said that the congregation who had worshipped in it from its first erection left it to a man and joined the Free Church; yet after they left, a new congregation was gradually collected to take possession of it. An adherent, Mr James Bogie, lately deceased, bestowed an annual endowment of £50 on it; but now we understand that it has been raised to the status of a *quod-sacra* church, its parish being the town of Pathhead and St Clairtown, that is, St Clairtown below the railway station. The chapel is a very substantial and convenient place of worship, but it is sadly encumbered by trees which have been planted round it, and which, besides, darken the windows very much. Sittings 950. Mr James B. Haxton became the minister in the year 1850.

There is also a small body of Baptists, who meet in Back Street Hall. This body was originally an offshoot from the Baptist congregation in Whyte's Causeway, Kirkcaldy, in 1855. They were soon after joined by another small body of similar views and practice, which had been worshipping for several years in the Links Meal Hall. After having occasion to shift their place of meeting several times, in 185–, they obtained a lease of their present house, and have fitted it up in a very commodious manner. Sittings about 140.

It is but doing justice to a considerable portion of
the inhabitants of Pathhead and St Clairtown, however, to remark, that besides the ample church accommodation to which we have already referred, there are
a very respectable number who attend regularly places
of worship not situated in the district. Thus, a very
considerable number of the members of the United
Presbyterian chapel at the east end of Kirkcaldy, which
was built in 1820, as already referred to, and now under
the pastoral care of Mr William Fleming, belong to
Pathhead and St Clairtown. And, moreover, when
the Burghers and Anti-burghers divided in 1747, as
also referred to in this section, a number of the former
lived in Pathhead and vicinity; of course they continued to attend their old place of worship, the " Links
Kirk," as before. Although the number of these is not
so great as it was sixty years ago, yet still it is very
respectable. " Our Harry," as the late Mr Shirra used
to term the precentor, (Henry Rait, sen.,) lived in
St Clairtown, directly opposite the Free Church. The
Links kirk was built in 1740, and Mr Shirra was
ordained in 1750. He left in 1798, and went to
Stirling, and died there in 1803. Mr Law succeeded
in 1799, and held the office until his death in 1859.
Having become infirm, in 1810 Mr J. B. Johnson
was inducted as his collegue and successor. Mr
Johnson left in 1854; and was succeeded by Mr
W. R. Thomson, who left in 1861. Mr Robert
Dick Brownlee, the present minister, was ordained in
November 1862. The original place of worship was
built in 1740, but in 1831 it was taken down and a
new one built a little farther to the northward. It is
quite a respectable looking building, both inside and

outside, and contains 1100 sittings. It is denominated "Bethelfield Church."

There are, besides, a few of the inhabitants of Pathhead who belong to the Congregational body in Cowan
Street, Kirkcaldy. There are also some who belong
to the Baptist congregation in Whyte's Causeway.

Altogether, it will be seen what an immense difference there is between the church accommodation which
the present generation in Pathhead, and, indeed, the
whole inhabitants of the parish of Dysart, enjoy, from
that which was the lot of our forefathers previous to
1747. Then, there was not a single place of worship
in the district; now, there are four well fitted up in the
district or close upon it. Then, there was only one
place of worship in the whole parish, and that one
small and inconvenient; now, there are eight, and another within a little distance. The difference is not
only very great in respect to the number of the sittings,
but also in respect to the very comfortable manner in
which places of worship are now fitted up. It is
within the recollection of the writer, when there was
not a particle of fire to be seen in any place of worship in this neighbourhood, even in the coldest day in
winter; now, they are all comfortably heated. Formerly there was not even provision made for lighting
with candles; now, they are all splendidly lighted with
gas. Ventilation in places of public concourse was not
then thought of, but now this matter has been satis-
factorily attended to, and everything that is calculated
to conduce to the comfort of the worshippers has been
secured.

## SUPERIORS OF DUNNIKIER.

There is one very important circumstance connected
with this part of our narrative which it is indispensable that our readers be made acquainted with, namely,
that previous to the Reformation the estate of Dunnikier belonged to the Church.   Hence it was denominated the " Kirklands of Dunnikier ; " in other words,
it formed a part of the extensive possessions of the
Abbey of Dunfermline.   This Abbey was one of the
richest, if not the very richest, in Scotland.   Thus
Musselburgh and Inveresk on the south side of the
Forth, and in Fife we find that Burntisland, Kinghorn,
Kirkcaldy, the lands of Balweary, Dunnikier, and a
number of other places, held of this Abbey.   The
abbots exercised an uncontrolled jurisdiction over these
towns and estates, more powerful, we believe, in one
respect, than that which any of the kings ever exercised, namely, that they gave tacks or leases for a
specified number of years, in the same manner as farms
are let to tenants now.

The first superior of Dunnikier that we have heard
of was killed at the disastrous battle of Flodden, when
James IV. and the flower of his army were cut off.
What was the name of this individual we have not
learned, but it would appear that previous to his setting out to join the army he had a certain forboding of
what awaited him, for he made his will, and by it
bequeathed a donation to the chapel of St Dennis in
Dysart, the last donation, it is said, that it ever received : the Reformation taking place a few years afterwards, all such gifts would cease.   It is probable,
however, that the name of this superior was John
Murray.   The battle of Flodden was fought in 1513,

and we find it recorded that just six years afterwards, that is, in 17th April 1519, "Marion Pitcairne, relict of the umpy John Murray of Newtown, of Markinch, assigned to Robert Pitcairne and his aires the sd. lands of Dunnikier, and to the tacks made to her, be Andrew, Archbishop of St Andrews, Abbot of Dunfermline, thereanent." It is therefore probable that this was the widow of him who fell at Flodden. The Abbot referred to here was Andrew Forman, who was in the see of St Andrews, and was, besides, perpetual commendator of Dunfermline Abbey from 1514 to 1522.

Next we have, under date of 1529, a tack of the said lands to Andrew Lundie, brother of James Lundie of Balgeny, for the space of eleven years, at the annual feu-duty of £8 Scots, granted by "James, Archbishop of St Andrews, Primate of Scotland, Administrator of the Monastrie of Dunfermline, with consent of George, Abbot of the said Monastrie and Convent." This archbishop was James Bethune of Balfour, and had the see from 1522 to 1539. He was uncle to the well-known David Bethune, who succeeded him, and who was made a cardinal. The abbot referred to here was George Durie, the last abbot of Dunfermline. He held the office from 1530, until the monastery and church were destroyed in 1560. He died in 1572.

Then, under date 16th October 1540:—"A tack sett to the said Andrew Lundie for nineteen years, at the same rate of feu-duty, by George, Archdeacone of St Andrews, Abbot of Dunfermline, with consent of the Convent." Next, we have an infeftment in favour of David Lundie of Balgeny, 1575. But notwithstanding of him being infeft in the estate, we find that Robert Pitcairne, commendator of Dunfermline, refused to grant him a charter, until the Court of Session, at the in-

stance of David Lundie, compelled him.   The charter
was signed March 15, 1576; but the feu-duty was
raised to £11, 4s. Scots.   Robert Pitcairne was appointed commendator in 1560, and held the office
until his death in 1584.   There were two other com-
mendators after that; but in 1589, James VI. converted
the abbey, with its lands and privileges, into a tempo-
ral lordship, and conferred it upon his queen, Anne of
Denmark.   The Hon. Robert Lundie succeeded his
father, Andrew Lundie, under a charter from Queen
Anne, with consent of her husband, James VI., of date
10th February 1593.   In 1608, he granted to the
feuars the privilege of taking "fale and dovat, clay and
querrel," from the Muir of Dunnikier.   His son, Robert
Lundie, jun., succeeded him, under charter from "Charles
I., then Prince of Scotland, Lord of the Lordships and
Regalitie of Dunfermline," &c., of date 11th May 1612.
On 16th February 1627, Robert Lundie made over the
lands of Dunnikier to James and David Boswel of the
West Mill.   In February 1630, these individuals made
over the estate to David Young.   In November 1648,
David Young sold the lands of Dunnikier to James
Law, burgess of Kirkcaldy.   We find next a disposition
of the said lands granted by James Law, with consent
of Agnes Durie, his spouse, and Alexander Law, his
son, and others, to John Watson, burgess of Burntisland.

In 1666, John Watson was engaged in a lawsuit
with the minister of Dysart about a glebe, and a decreet
was given the same year.   It should here be mentioned that, although there are abundance of papers
connected with this matter in existence, yet it is almost
impossible to read them ; but we learn from the burgh
books of Dysart that, in the year 1635, Dr Mitchelson,

minister of Burntisland, designed a glebe of $4\frac{1}{2}$ acres, of the kirk lands of Dunnikier, to Mr Nairne, minister of Dysart. How it happened that a minister of Burnt-island should take it upon him to give away to any party a portion of the lands of Dunnikier we have no means of knowing, but it is probable that the minister of Dysart was pursuing John Watson for this glebe of $4\frac{1}{2}$ acres. It must be noted, however, that Mr Nairne was dead before the lawsuit commenced; and as there was then, as now, two ministers in Dysart, we do not know the name of the individual who claimed the glebe. But be that as it may, it is very evident that he lost the plea; for, in the first place, there is not the slightest evidence to prove that any minister of Dysart ever had possession of any portion of the lands of Dunnikier as a glebe. And, second, it is equally evident that there never was any acknowledgment, in a money payment, by the superiors of Dunnikier to the minister, in lieu of the glebe; for there are in exist-ence a number of receipts, granted by the ministers of Dysart to the proprietors of Dunnikier, both a number of years before and a number of years after the law-suit in question, and they are all, without exception, of the same value—namely, £200 Scots annually.

In the same year, 1666, John Watson was the pur-suer in an action before the Court of Session with his feuars; but we forbear saying anything about the matter, as we have referred to it already in another part of our work. In July 1684, he made the first grant of burying-ground to the inhabitants of Dunni-kier. On September 10, same year, Wodrow, in his "History of the Church of Scotland," says, "John Watson and his spouse were fined £1050 for *irregu-larities*,"—that is, we presume, not attending the preach-

ing of the curates regularly. On 24th December, same
year, John Watson and Euphan Orrock, his spouse,
purchased from Alexander Ayton, of Inchdairnie, certain parts and portions of his lands, for their own liferent, and mortified them in favour of the master of the
grammar school, and three poor widows; registered in
the Burgh Court books of Burntisland, September 17,
1694. Again: Disposition and deed of mortification
by John Watson, Esq., of Dunnikier, of a tenement of
land in Burntisland, in favour of Euphan Orrock, his
spouse, in liferent, for the residence of three poor
widows; dated 5th May 1689, and registered in Burgh
Court books of Burntisland, 15th January 1776. The
reader will find a circumstantial account of these mor-
tifications in the Statistical Account of Scotland: Burntisland. Again, on 16th November 1689, John Watson granted a disposition to John Watson, son of
Captain John Watson of Leith, his cousin, and Euphan
Orrock, his spouse, and their heirs, of the estate of
Dunnikier, and also a tenement in Burntisland. The
wording of this will (which we have seen) is somewhat
remarkable. It states in the commencement, (we quote
from memory,) that having no children of his own, he
wished to leave his property to one of his relations,
the most deserving of them, and particularly to those
of them who bore the surname of Watson; and the
reason why he singled out this John Watson and
Euphan Orrock, his spouse, was because they had
married with his consent and full contentment, &c.;
and it rather appears that the wife of the heir was a
relation of his own wife, being of the same name.
There is an obscure hint following, which bears this
interpretation. John Watson died January 6, 1694.

In the year 1695, July 17, John Watson, jun.,

obtained an Act of Parliament, authorising the holding
of two annual fairs in the town of Dunnikier, to continue three days each. This was a privilege of great
importance in those days; although, from the great
changes which have taken place in Scottish society
since that time, such fairs are of no value now; yea,
rather, are positively injurious to those who frequent
them. On 5th October 1703, he sold the estate to
Captain James Oswald, of Kirkcaldy, for 45,000 merks,
and we have no doubt that he was compelled by
sheer necessity to do so. Towards the conclusion of
his possession of the estate he had fallen deeply in
debt. We have seen a list of a great number of bonds
which he had given for small sums of money, which he
had borrowed from persons residing in the neighbourhood. It is remarkable that all these bonds are dated
as late as 1700, and from that year down to the sale
of the estate in October 1703. The sum total of these
bonds was 37,778 merks. Captain Oswald, in pur-
chasing the estate, took upon himself the whole responsibility of this debt, and granted an obligation to that
effect to John Watson.

Captain James Oswald appears to have been a native
of Kirkcaldy, for several of his relations were burgesses
and even magistrates of that burgh. He was himself
Provost of Kirkcaldy. In the year 1681 he had a
grant of a coat of arms from Sir Alexander Erskine,
Lord Lyon King-of-Arms. He sat in the last Scottish
Parliament as representative of Kirkcaldy. He had a
vessel which appears to have been engaged principally
in trading to Holland or to other places on the continent, and to have brought home a great variety of
goods on his own account, which he sold to those who
required them. We have now before us an account,

extending from July 15, 1708, to June 24, 1713, of
his against a Christian Hutchison, relict of James Hay,
in which there are various articles mentioned, which
were supplied by him, the greater part of which, at
least, appear to have been imported from abroad. Thus,
there are nine ells, slates, tiles, linen, harn, lint, dye-
stuffs, &c., to be found in this account, amounting in
value (including money lent) to £239, 16s. 6d. Scots.
It is very probable that it was him who built the
mansion in Kirkcaldy, and in which the family continued
to reside until about 1790, when James Townsend
Oswald built Dunnikier House.  He died in the year
1724.

Captain Oswald's only son, James Oswald, died
before his father, and thus did not come into the possession of the estate.  He married Anna Durie, daughter of John Durie, of Letham, Provost of Kirkcaldy, by
whom he had four sons : James, John, Thomas, and
another, name unknown.

The Right Honourable James Oswald was born in
1715, and succeeded Captain Oswald, his grandfather,
as proprietor of Dunnikier.  He had lost his father at
a very early age, yet his mother, Anna Durie, commonly called "the Lady of Dunnikier," who was a very
active and sharp-sighted woman, cultivated his talents
with the greatest care and assiduity, and gave him the
best education which Scotland could then afford, and
even sent him abroad to improve his mind.  We have
seen a feu-charter simply signed Anna Durie, in 1737,
at which time we suppose he must have been on his
travels abroad.  She indeed, it is said, planned and
superintended everything connected with the estate.
He became an advocate about 1740, although there
is no evidence extant to shew that he ever practised

at the Scottish bar. His mother was particularly anxious to see him introduced into Parliament, in the firm belief that there he would have full exercise for his superior talents. In 1741 he was elected representative for the Kirkcaldy district of burghs, and he was successively elected in the same district, or in the county of Fife, until, being attacked with a very grievous malady, broken down in body and in mind, he was compelled to resign in 1768. He filled successively the offices of Commissioner of the Navy, Lord of Trade and Plantations, Lord of the Treasury, and Treasurer of Ireland ; he was also a member of the Privy Council, and was made a Right Honourable in 1760 ; and it was anticipated by his friends that, if bad health had not unfortunately cut short his public career, he would in due time have become Chancellor of the Exchequer.

It is related of him by Dr Carlyle, in his autobiography, that about the year 1758, he happened to be in London when the Parliament was sitting, and being anxious to hear Mr Pitt, he went to the House of Commons one day when a certain debate came on, in which that celebrated statesman took an active part. Several members who took an opposite view of the case from him, attacked him, but he did not condescend to answer any of them, excepting Mr James Oswald. Sir John Oswald, his grandson, who in the year 1825 published *a portion* of his correspondence, (a great part having been accidentally destroyed by fire,) states, that although he was not a frequent speaker in Parliament, yet he was always an effective and powerful one. He was honoured by the friendship and correspondence of some of the greatest and most talented men of his day. He had three brothers, as we have already said ; the first, John, was successively Rector of Rode, Prebend of

Westminster, and Bishop of Raphoe, in Ireland. The second, Thomas, was a colonel in the army. What became of the youngest, or what was his name, we have not learned. We have seen a feu-charter granted by James, at Wandsworth in Surrey, 1740, in which all the three brothers names occur, he as principal, and his two brothers as witnesses.

The Right Honourable Mr James Oswald died in 1770, and was succeeded by his only child, James Townsend Oswald, Esq., who was born in 1748. He sat one session in Parliament as representative for the Kirkcaldy district of burghs. In 1792 he concluded a bargain with the feuars regarding the Muir, as recorded in another part of this work. His daughter Elizabeth was married to the late Earl of Elgin in 1810, and was mother of the present Earl, at present Governor-General of India. James Townsend Oswald died in 1813.

Sir John Oswald, K.C.B., succeeded his father, J. T. Oswald, as proprietor of the estate of Dunnikier. He was born in 1771, entered the army as second lieutenant in 1788, and was made lieutenant in 1789. In 1791, he obtained a captain's commission; in July 1793, he was brigade-major to General Leland. He was present at the capture of the islands of Martinique, St Lucie, and Guadaloupe, and was personally engaged in all the various actions connected therewith. In 1797 he was appointed lieutenant-colonel in the 35th Foot; and in 1799 embarked in the expedition to Holland, and on the 19th September his first battalion was long and severely engaged, and sustained great loss. He was particularly thanked by the Duke of Gloucester, to whose brigade he belonged; but he was severely wounded, and had to return to England for the re-

covery of his health. In 1800 he embarked for the
Mediterranean, and was present at the blockade and
capture of Malta. In 1805 he had the brevet of
colonel; when the troops landed in Sicily, he was
appointed commandant of Melazzo; he afterwards
commanded the advance guard destined to cover the
disembarkation of the troops in St Eufemia Bay;
defeated with great loss a considerable body of the
enemy; was appointed to the third brigade of that
army, and commanded the same at the battle of
Maida; the siege of Scylla Castle was intrusted to him,
and after twenty days' resistance it was subdued. In 1807
he went into Egypt, under the orders of Major-General
Fraser, and was engaged in very laborious and successful service there. In 1808 he was made brigadier-
general in the Mediterranean, and commanded the expedition to the Ionian Islands, which surrendered to the
troops under his orders, and was, in addition to mili
tary duties, charged with the whole administration of
the different islands. On the 4th June 1811, he was
raised to the rank of major-general; went to the
Peninsula the same year, and was very actively engaged there, and particularly at the battle of Vittoria,
and the siege of St Sebastian; but in the end of 1812,
or beginning of 1813, family affairs compelled him to
return to Britain.

He was twice honoured with his sovereign's gracious
acknowledgment of services in which he held chief
command, and three times for those in which he held
a subordinate station; twice by name he received the
thanks of Parliament, and was also nominally included
in the vote for the battle of Maida. He bore three
medals—one for Maida, one for Vittoria, and one for
the siege of St Sebastian. He was Knight Grand Cross

of the Bath, and Knight Grand Cross of St Michael and St George. He was made lieutenant-general in 1819, and general in 1837. He died in 1840, and was succeeded by his son, James Townsend Oswald, as proprietor of Dunnikier.

## OFFICIALS.

Pathhead is what is denominated a " barony,"—that is, an estate holding of the Crown. Feu-duty is paid by the feuars to the superior for the respective feus which they hold of him. In all the old charters granted to them, there was a clause inserted, binding them to appear three times in the year at what were termed the " Head Courts," or any other courts which the superior might think proper to hold; and at one of these Head Courts held in 1722, it was enacted that every absentee should be fined half a merk, orders being given to the ground-officer to poind if the fine was not paid. But it would appear that even at that period the feuars considered the calling them out and causing them to answer to their names three times a year, was an unnecessary and useless stretch of authority. And so lax were they in their attendance, and so persistent was the laird in the exercise of his prerogative, that in course of a few years the fine was doubled. However, these Head Courts appear to have died a natural death towards the end of last century; there is no trace of them after the time of Bailie Alexander Grieg.

The superior presided at the courts; but if he should happen to be absent, the bailie supplied his place. He was appointed by the superior, and was simply his deputy, having full power to act in every instance in court, or out of it, with the same authority as the superior himself would have exercised if he were present. All criminal cases were brought before the courts, and the parties found guilty were generally fined, more or less, according to the degree of their guilt.

In the early part of last century, various enactments were made by the superior for the good of the town, and for restraining the careless and lawless; and the bailie was armed with full power to see the enactments carried out. Thus, on March 19, 1722, at a Head Court, "it was enacted and ordained, and hereby ordaine, all or every persone or persones who have ocassione to build houses or stairs, or any other building fronting to the fore street, to apply to the said Thomas Grieg, Baillie, before they lay the foundation, that he may approve thereof, under the penalty of thrie pund scotts." "July 11, 1734.—The Baillie, considering the many abuses and disturbance that is committed under cloud of night, by apprentices, servants, and young people, which is chiefly ocassioned by masters of families not taking due care and inspection over their families in keeping regular hours: Therefore the Baillie enacts, whatever apprentice, servant, or young person shall be found guilty of keeping irregular hours or making any disturbance in the night time, each parent or master shall be lyable for their children, apprentices, or servants, for what fines shall be inflicted or imposed upon them." "It is also enacted that no heritor, within the town, shall sett any house to, and receive any of his neighbour heritors' tenants into any house or houses, ay and untill the first master or heritor be paid of his bygone house-rents, which if any do, in the contrair, they shall be lyable to the former heritor in what rents shall be found due by the tennant. It is furder enacted, that no inhabitant in this town shall conceall on the mercat-day any cloath, lint, or wool, or other mercat goods, to the prejudice of the customer, his custom of such goods, with certification, the person guilty shall not only be liable in what custom such goods, but also in the sum of forty shillings scots for each transgression." "Feb. 7, 1735.—And siclike the said Alexander Philp (Arthur's neuk) has been in use, and practice, for these two or three years past, to keep ane big midden upon the high street opposite his own door, which is so big, that it stagnates the water coming from the west, and makes a great myre or puddle, which makes that part of the street impassable for any person on foot, unless they wyde through gutters, to the hurt and prejudice of the haill adjacent neighbours, heritors, and tenants, and all passengers passing that way, and obliges people either to go to the nether street, or west by the back of the town, when they would go through the over street, which is a delay to the haill residenters in the over street, notwithstanding the said Alexander Philp has been several times ordered and desired to remove said midden. Ordaines the said Alexander Philp, defender, to remove the midden opposite to his door, at or before Wednesday nixt at twelve o'clock, midday, under the penalty of five pounds scots for the first fault, ten pound for the second, fifteen pound for the third, and so proportionally more for each transgression so committed by him in time coming. Tho. Grieg." "25 November 1736.—There being a complaint made by several of the heritors, that several of the heritors and inhabitants of laying down their muck and making middens on the hie street, which stops the common passage ; Dunnikier and his Baillie do hereby enact and ordain, that no heritor or inhabitant in Dunnikier make any middings, or throw out any muck or smiddy-ashes on the hie street in time coming, under the penalty of five pounds scots for each transgression; and whatever muck shall be laid down by any person on the street in order to carry it to their land, that such person or persons shall carry off the same within twenty-four hours after the same is laid down, under the penalty of five pounds scots.                     " JAMES OSWALD.

THO. GRIFG."

There having been a great deal of discussion in various courts anent some of the feuars letting their houses to improper persons, we find, on Oct. 7, 1741, the following enactment :—" Ordaines that the haill feuars in Dunnikier give in a list of their haill tennents' names twixt and the first day of December nixt, so that the tennents may be known, and vagrants turned out of town, and that under the penalty of three pounds scots for each feuar neglecting."

There are various other laws recorded which relate to persons trespassing upon their neighbours' lands ; boys pulling pease on the land, or from stacks, &c. ; but we suppose we have given a sufficient number of quotations already.   We shall just give one more extract :—" Nov. 2, 1744—Ordaines all persons that keeps hens or cocks within the town, that they clip one of their foulls' wings, so thereby prevent their foulls from fleeing upon their neighbours' houses, and destroy the thaking, or destroy the thaking of their neighbours' stalks, and that under the penalty of forty shillings scots for each transgression."   " And there being a complaint made that several persons not only dress their lint in fire-houses, and at night makes use of candles in dressing their lint, and, when done, throws down the pob or brock of their lint into the open street, near houses that is thackt, and near cornbarnes and yairds : therefore Dunnikier and his Baillie prohibits and discharges all persons within this town, from dressing their lint in any house where there is fire, and that they make use of no candle when dark in dressing their lint; and also prohibits and discharges all persons from laying down pob or dightings of their lint into any street near thatcht houses, cornbarnes or yairds, so that neighbours may be kept safe from the danger of fire or other inconveniency, and that under the penalty of ten pounds scots for each transgression.

" JAMES OSWALD.

THO. GRIEG, Baillie."

We here see that if the inhabitants of this town were not kept within the bounds of decorum, it was not for want of legislation.

We have already seen how important the office of bailie was, during the first half of last century, in reference to criminal matters ; but we find that he was of equal importance in regard to civil transactions. Thus we find, for instance, that, in the year 1731, a complaint was made to the bailie, Thomas Grieg, by a tenant, that the house in which he was residing stood in very much need of being repaired, and petitioning him to exercise his authority in causing it to be repaired out of the rents,—several heirs being connected with the house at the time. This complaint having been made, the bailie and two of the burliemen went and inspected the house, and ordered the necessary repairs to be made forthwith. Again, in 1754, a petition was presented to the bailie, Alexander Grieg, in regard to the same property, by Alexander Grieg, who lived in Kennoway Burns, who had lately come into possession of the property, setting forth that a certain tenant in the house was going to remove, and as he had not paid the rent, he requests the bailie to employ a competent person to seize as much of the goods or furniture of the tenant as would pay the rent, and roup the said goods publicly for that purpose. The bailie accordingly complied with this request.

The bailies were chosen for life. We have not been able to ascertain when they were first appointed in this town. Until very lately, it was indispensable that a bailie should be present on the ground when an infeftment was taken; but it is a well-known fact, that any person might be appointed to act for the time being. In a number of the very old infeftments that we have seen, we find the names of individuals inserted as bailies who belonged to Kirkcaldy, or other places in the neighbourhood. The first regular baron bailie that we have any certain information about, was John Thomson, who was in the office in 1698, or perhaps earlier, and continued to act until 1719, when it is probable he resigned in consequence of old age. He died on one of the fast-days of 1727. He was succeeded by Thomas Grieg, who retained the office until his death, which took place in 1751. His son, Alexander Grieg, succeeded him, and held the office until some time between 1786 and 1791, when he obtained a situation in the Excise, and left the town; but in a few years after, he was superannuated, and died in Kirkcaldy, somewhere in the neighbourhood of the

present Custom-House, in 1800.    James Anderson
succeeded him as bailie, and exercised the office until
his death in 1815.    David Inglis was the next bailie;
he died in 1832, and was succeeded by Charles Walker,
who died in 1853.    The office has not been filled up
since his death.    What the reason is for this neglect
we do not know.    Whatever may be said about the
police supplying the place of the bailie in regard to
criminal matters, we are decidedly of opinion that
there is no one to supply his place in regard to the
settling of differences between individual feuars and
marches.    In reference to such matters, the bailie
was assisted by four individuals, who were termed Burliemen, or perhaps more properly, Birlawmen.    These
officials were chosen by the superior, or by the bailie,
and on entering upon office, took the oath *de fidele*.
They were originally appointed for one year only, but
afterwards their term of office was extended to two
years ; but it was afterwards extended to their life-
time, or until they were incapacitated by infirmity or
old age.    During last century, there were also two
individuals elected annually, who were termed Quar-
termasters, whose duty it was to regulate the billeting
of soldiers on the inhabitants.    And moreover, lastly,
there were also appointed four individuals, who were
termed Visitors, and whose duty it was to inspect flesh,
meal, and other *vivers*, to see that they were whole-
some; and also to inspect bauks, broads, and weights.
In case of the visitors finding any deficiency in regard
to any of those matters, they reported the same to the
bailie, who called the guilty parties before him, and
fined them more or less according to the extent of their
criminality.

The following is the list of individuals who have

filled the office of Boxmaster or Preses, as far as can be ascertained, during the last seventy years :—

| | | | |
|---|---|---|---|
| Mr David Millie filled the office in 1792 and 1793. | | | |
| Messrs Michael Duff, | elected | 1802 | |
| ... Andrew Haggart, | ... | 1804 | |
| ... David Forgan, | ... | 1807 | |
| ... David Inglis, | ... | 1808 | |
| ... David Millie, jun., | ... | 1810 | |
| ... Andrew Forgan, | ... | 1817 | |
| ... Alexander Grieg, | ... | 1820 | |
| ... Alexander Beveridge, | ... | 1825 | |
| ... David Bogie, | ... | 1827 | |
| ... Michael Duff, | ... | 1830 | |
| ... John Lornie, | ... | 1832 | |
| ... William Fair, | ... | 1836 | |
| ... John Grieg, | ... | 1838 | |
| ... William Pringle, | ... | 1840 | |
| ... Robert Grieg, | ... | 1842 | |
| ... James Pringle, | ... | 1852 | |
| ... John Kay, | ... | 1854 | |

## HOUSES, FEU-DUTIES, AND RENTS.

The original houses in Pathhead had, with very few exceptions, thatched roofs, and a considerable number of them were only one story high. Many of them were built with clay, lime being very scarce and dear. The clay, no doubt, was obtained partly from the Muir; but there was originally a clay-hole within the town, namely, in that spot which, within these last few years, has been dignified with the title of " Arthur's Neuk ;" however, by the end of the seventeenth century, the ground was feued, and a house, the present one, we presume, built. The feu-duty, which is paid to the superior, is, we suppose, precisely what it was two hundred years ago, namely, 13s. Scots for each rood. But a feuing rood is a very indefinite idea, the front varying from 22 or 23 feet to nearly 30. A feu of such a frontage on the north side of the Nether Street, and reaching to the Mid Street, was counted a rood and a-half; while one of a similar description on the north side of the Mid Street, not being of such a length as the former, was only reckoned a single rood. A very great change has taken place in the value of property since the town was first feued, and especially since the middle of last century. Since the last-mentioned period, the value of property has increased threefold, and of course rents have increased in like proportion. In 1703, the estate of Dunnikier was purchased by Captain James Oswald from John Watson for 45,000 merks, just £2500 sterling. In 1648, the rent of the estate was 2000 merks, or £111, 2s. 2d. In 1702, the farm of Overtown was let for a term of thirteen years, at an annual rent of 8 bolls bear, 30 bolls oats, and 100 merks Scots. Of course, a very great rise in the value of the estate has taken place since that period, and the rents have risen in proportion. The very same remark will apply to house property in the town. Of course, the same rise in the value of property of every kind has taken place through the whole country.

---

## MONEY.

Accounts were universally reckoned in Scots money in this place, down to the middle of the last century. The people sometimes spoke of pounds when referring to a sum of money, but as often they reckoned by merks. The pound Scots was just 20 pence sterling, and a merk two-thirds of a pound, or $13\frac{1}{3}$ pence. And

although *all* accounts were reckoned by sterling money
long before 1800, yet we have often heard old people,
a considerable time after this century had begun, talk-
ing about twal pennies when they just meant one
penny sterling. It is not easy to root out old customs
which have been universal in a community.

## ANNUAL FAIRS.

An Act of the Scottish Parliament, dated July 17,
1695, appointed two annual fairs to be held in the
town of Pathhead, each fair to last for three days.
Since the alteration of the style in 1753, the fairs
have been held on the first Wednesday and Thursday
of August, and the 7th of October. We subjoin a list
of customs charged by the superior in last century,
*Scots money* :—

|  | s. | d. |
|---|---|---|
| For ilk pack of south country wooll, | 6 | 8 |
| For each fardel of south country wooll, | 4 | 0 |
| For ilk stone of Fyfe wooll of customs, | 1 | 4 |
| For weighing ilk stone of Fyfe wooll, | 0 | 6 |
| For ilk stone of wooll of tollpenie, | 0 | 8 |
| For ilk stone of lint of custome, | 1 | 6 |
| For weighing ilk stone of lint, | 0 | 6 |
| For ilk stone of lint of tollpenie, | 0 | 8 |
| For ilk stone of lining-cloath of custome, | 1 | 6 |
| For ilk ox or cow that comes to be sold, | 2 | 0 |
| For ilk ox or cow of tollpenie that is sold, | 1 | 0 |
| For ilk drapster for custome, | 1 | 0 |
| For ilk peutherer for custome, and stand, | 6 | 0 |
| For ilk cordiner's stand, | 2 | 0 |
| For ilk chapman's closs stand and custome, | 2 | 0 |
| For ilk chapman's open stand upon a stool, or stool length, and custome, | 0 | 6 |
| For a merchant's stand, being a deal-length, | 4 | 0 |
| For ilk load of wheat bread, | 2 | 0 |

|  | s. | d. |
|---|---|---|
| For ane horse-load of cooper work, | 2 | 0 |
| For ane horse-load of caps, | 2 | 0 |
| For a load or parcell of sives and riddels, | 1 | 0 |
| For a load of cans or pegs, | 2 | 0 |
| For a horse-load of barrows, shovels, &c., | 4 | 0 |
| For a horse-load of strings, | 0 | 6 |
| For a horse-load of lining-cloath of tollpenie, | 2 | 0 |
| For a fardell or half a load of lining-cloath of tollpenie, | 1 | 0 |
| For a codwair-full of lining-cloath of tollpenie, | 0 | 6 |
| For each spainell of yairn, | 0 | 2 |
| For each gallon of ale coming into the town, | 0 | 6 |
| For each web of check or bengall, | 2 | 0 |
| For each horse-load of fruit, | 1 | 0 |

The customs of the two markets were rouped every year, and sold to the highest bidder. It would appear, that generally, if not always, it was feuars who bid for them, and obtained them. The successful bidder had always to obtain another individual to be his cautioner; but it was very probable that the bidder and the cautioner were equally interested in the matter. These customs generally fetched £6 or £7 sterling, and even in one year, namely 1740, they brought £9, 10s.; this was, of course, for both markets.

Although, strictly speaking, this work is merely historical, yet we cannot avoid pausing, and making one or two remarks for the consideration of the reader. First, in looking over the above list of articles upon which custom was levied in this town, it is worthy of notice that these articles were all necessaries of life, or at least considered as such in old times, with the exception of two items, namely, drapsters' stands and fruit. This shews at once what kinds of goods were expected to be in the market. People living in the vicinity, yea, and individuals living in the country, expected such articles to be in the market, and came to buy accordingly. In bygone times this resorting to markets was not merely a convenience, but a necessity, for the shops were very few in number, and those few very scantily furnished. Second, it is plain, from the large amount of money that the customs realised, that a very considerable quantity of goods must have been sold. This shews us that in those days markets, such as those of Pathhead were, were both useful and necessary. But, third, it is easily seen that the character of the markets is entirely changed now. With the exception of shoes and cooper work, and perhaps pewterer's ware, none of the articles specified in the above table are now to be seen in our markets. People do not come to the markets now to buy articles of necessity, and accordingly none are exposed for sale. The reason why people do not come to markets looking for cloth and other articles specified in the above table, is simply this, that there are now in every town numerous and well-furnished shops, where goods of every description and in endless variety are to be had *every day* for ready money, and even in some instances on credit. The inference to be naturally drawn from these remarks is just this, that as the markets do not answer the end now for which they were originally established, they ought to be abolished. There cannot be a doubt that in 1695, when John Watson, jun., obtained the Act of Parliament for establishing the markets in this town, the inhabitants would be very grateful for the boon, for boon it was at that period ; but now the privilege has become a nuisance. The markets are not merely unnecessary but pernicious. It would contribute very much to the health and morality of the community if these markets were abolished altogether. It does not appear that they ever extended to the Parliamentary maximum of three days, at least we have never heard of such a thing. The August market was, as far back as we have heard about it, kept for two days, but the Wednesday was generally confined to the sale of shoes, while Thursday was the real fair day for the sale of everything else that was wanted by those who frequented then. But now of late years the October market has vanished altogether; it never lasted more than one day as far as our personal knowledge extends, and two or three drapsters' stands being all the affair. In regard to the August market again, a number of years ago the Wednesday sale of shoes was shifted from Nether Street to Mid Street, on account of the number of stage coaches which were at that time running on the former all hours of the day. Since that time, however, it has gradually dwindled away, so that we may say that it has gone into oblivion like the October one. There are, however, a few stands with shoes to be seen in the Mid Street in the early part of Thursday, so that now there is only one market day in the year, instead of six as appointed by Act of Parliament. Merry-go-rounds, and caravans, and confectionary, and such like plans for fleecing the lieges of their money, are to be found in all their varieties on this one day in this town, much the same as in other towns in Scotland; and, as we said before, the sooner this day is abolished the better, although, we confess, there is no prospect of that at present.

Quite in keeping with what we have already said about the shops in this neighbourhood, both as regards their small number, and, in general, their meagre supply of goods, we may remind our readers that in this place there were in former times, and within our own remembrance, certain females who made a living by going to Leith every week by the passage-boats from Kirkcaldy, and bringing over quantities of sugar, tea, quartern loaves, barrels of salt herrings, &c., which were not to be obtained readily in any other way by families on this side of the water. These articles were retailed by those individuals to those who wanted them, and their returning from Edinburgh was generally anxiously looked for, and the goods which they brought with them did not lie on their hand, but were eagerly bought up.

## MODE OF ADVERTISING GOODS FOR SALE.

It is very remarkable that there does not appear to have been any change in this respect for the last 150 years, or perhaps since the town was first built. The two methods now in use were in use as far back as we have any certain knowledge of the matter, namely, the drum and the clap or bell. The " clap" will be remembered by many of our readers as being an article somewhat like an old tin canister, about six or seven inches in length, and four or five in breadth, open at one of the ends, with a small tongue in it, similar to that of a bell. This article was used on *ordinary* occasions, such as advertising the sale of beef, meal, &c., but the drum was only made use of for calling public meetings, advertising public roups of furniture, &c., just as at present. The "clap"—we believe the identical article which was in use down to the year 1828, (it being superseded by a new bell, Jan. 1, 1829)—is referred to as far back as Oct. 8, 1737, at a Head Court of Dunnikier :—" Dunnikier and his Baillie having heard the complaint of several of the heritors of the New Street that the clap does not come to sd. street

and give the common advertisement; Therefore ordaines
the clapman in time coming to pass through the New
Street and give the common proclamation and cries,
and appoints twelve pennies Scots to be the clapman's
wages to be payed by the inhabitants for each crye, and
eighteen pennis for each stranger." Notice of the
existence of the drum is still more ancient: it was repeatedly mentioned in the Head Courts, as being ordered
to be used for the purpose of announcing to the inhabitants the enactments of said courts. In the Burial-
Yard Cash-Book the following entry occurs:—" Dis-
bursed by me, Henry Reid, 8th Sept. 1718, To John
Thomson for mending the drum "—we have forgot the
sum. This shews that the drum had been for some
time in use. This John Thomson was, we believe, the
blue-gown of that name who lived in the town.
These blue-gowns had been made for the first time
shortly before the period here referred to, that is, in the
reign of Queen Anne. The town-drummer, we are led
to believe, was at the same time grave-digger and
ground-officer, and was appointed by the superior or
the bailie.

Connected with advertising, we may now refer to
the very solemn announcement which was made in the
olden time in this place by the grave-digger when a
funeral was to take place. There were no funeral letters issued in these days among the working classes—
not even a list of names drawn up of persons to be invited to attend the remains of their friends and ac-
quaintances to the narrow house, as at present: the
grave-digger did the whole in a very simple manner.
We have in our eye at present John Balfour, the last
official who invited the inhabitants to attend funerals in
the manner we are going to describe. He was a short

stout man with a large nose, and wore a short coat
with broad tails, such as is worn by some persons at
the present day. On the day previous to that appointed for the funeral taking place, he brought out his
bell and commenced his labours at the end of a street,
keeping his left hand under the tail of his coat, while
he held the bell in his right hand close to his thigh,
making a monotonous tinkling noise with it, and at
every little distance in the street he stopped and made
a proclamation somewhat in the following terms:—
"Our brother John Tosh has departed, and is to be
buried the morn at two o'clock, and it's expected that
you'll a' attend at the next warnin' o' the bell." Then
on the following day, immediately before the funeral
taking place, he went the same round as before, tinkling
the bell, but making no proclamation, always ending at
the door of the house where the corpse was lying; and
when the funeral lifted, he marched at the head of the
procession, carrying his bell by the tongue, with both
hands behind his back, all the way to the burying-
ground. As we have said, he was the last official who
went through these ceremonies. He died in June 1800,
at the age of eighty years. Let our readers remember that
it was not a "clap" which John made use of, but a true
and veritable bell. Some years after his death, a certain teacher in the town school had it fixed up on the
top of the school-house for warning out the scholars at
the appointed time; but it not being properly secured,
it fell to the ground and was broken. We believe that
the remains are still in existence in the neighbourhood.

The male inhabitants of the town responded to the
grave-digger's call quite readily, generally in their
working-clothes; the nailers with their leather aprons,
a great coat being added to hide all deficiencies; and

sometimes, we have been told, they appeared with nightcaps on their heads. But this neglect of dress would have the good effect of insuring a better attendance on these occasions than otherwise would have been the case. We may here remark, that black was by no means a fashionable colour in those days. The black clothes lay at the bottom of the chest, and were only brought out when necessity called for it. The ordinary wear of decent church-going people was almost every colour that can be conceived of, except black or red. And further, we may add that their Sunday clothes lasted for a very long period. They were made of a far more durable material than any cloth that is manufactured now.

The people in this place in bygone times were as tenacious in keeping up old customs, however unreasonable they might be, as the inhabitants of other districts. Thus in regard to funerals, of which we have just been speaking, for instance. An acquaintance of ours, who died at a good old age some years ago, informed us that when he first came to the town, it was the custom that when a person died in the west end of the Nether Street, they would not carry the corpse west, as being the nearest road to the burying-ground, although the footpath which had been originally there had been transformed into the Plantin Wynd, but they went east the Nether Street, up the Flesh Wynd, and then west the Mid Street. However, one day when a funeral was to take place from the west end of the street, he and two or three more individuals, who were determined to upset this superstitious custom, took hold of the spokes, and carried the corpse west the street and up the Plantin Wynd, and this has been the practice ever since.

## WITCHES.

We may here say a very few words about witches. In former times, the town of Pathhead was not a hairbreadth behind other towns in regard to the belief of the inhabitants in the existence and power of witches during last century, and even in the beginning of the present one; there were always some aged females who were reputed " *no canny,*" but there were others about whom the populace entertained no doubt whatever that they were true and veritable witches, in close league with his Satanic majesty. One of the most noted of these was Helen Smith, (*vulgo*, Witch Helen,) who died in 1776. Her exit from the world was a very remarkable and a very indecorous one. When the corpse was brought out of the house in order to be carried to the graveyard for interment, a number of boys who had entered into a combination for the purpose of giving her a singular funeral, seized hold of the spokes, and ran with her the whole of the way to the burying ground, followed by a number more, cheering vociferously all the way. But there were no police in those days, or such a scene could not have been witnessed. The witches have all disappeared from this quarter now. The schoolmaster is abroad.

## TRADE AND WAGES.

The principal occupation in Pathhead in olden times was that of nail-making. It appears from the best accounts we have of the nailers or " hammermen," as they were termed, that they formed the most numerous class in this locality. They must have turned out an immense number of nails in the course of a year. We have seen statements about this in various public documents, all copied from each other; but we do not think that it was possible, in the circumstances, to make any calculation on the subject that could be depended on. Until the latter part of the last century, all the nails manufactured in this neighbourhood were made from old iron. This iron was gathered in the neighbourhood; and it came, indeed, from all parts of the country, but we believe that the greater part of it came from Holland and other parts of the Continent. Previous to the French Revolution, there was a very brisk trade between the seaports of the Firth of Forth and Holland. This was particularly the case in regard to those ports in the Firth that exported coals and salt. In those days the Scotch had privileges in regard to trade with Holland, which the inhabitants of no other country possessed. For instance, at Campvere,* which is a town situated on the north side of the island of Walcheren, the same island that Flushing stands on, there was a gate called the *Scotch gate*, where the Scotch sailors got in free, while other sailors had to pay a small coin for admittance. Hence the expression "*Scot free*" took its rise from this privilege. So important were these privileges considered by the old Scottish Government, that an official was appointed to

* The intercourse between Scotland and the Low Countries, as they were called, commenced as early as the reign of Robert Bruce. The city of Bruges had a very large share of the trade for a long period; but the town of Campvere, although a small place, yet being more convenient and easy of access, and besides being at no great distance from the large and thriving city of Antwerp, in course of time drew away the trade from Bruges, which in consequence became almost deserted, and its numerous warehouses left empty.

look after them; he was dignified with the title of Lord Conservator of Scots Privileges at Campvere.* This office was conferred by the British Government on the celebrated John Home, the author of the tragedy of "Douglas," in the year 1758. By this time, however, it was merely a sinecure; the salary about £100.

The town of Pathhead was admirably situated for enjoying a share of the Dutch trade, having the port of Dysart, about three-quarters of a mile distant, on the one side, and Kirkcaldy, about a quarter of a mile distant, on the other—both of these ports sending considerable quantities of coals and salt to Holland. And among the various kinds of merchandise which the Scotch vessels brought back from that country was great quantities of old iron, out of which the nails were manufactured. This trade, of course, entirely ceased when the ports of Holland were shut against our vessels shortly before the battle of Camperdown, in 1797. This circumstance, no doubt, operated very disadvantageously on the nail-makers in this neighbourhood. But it was not the want of material altogether that caused the decline of this trade, but what may seem, at first sight, quite paradoxical; it was the introduction of a material already prepared for the workman which was the principal cause. The Carron Company, which had been established in 1760, carried on the manufacture of iron on a most extensive scale. Almost everything in that line they attempted, and successfully executed. And, among other articles, they prepared rods of a requisite thickness for the manufacture of nails, making them up, in bundles of 56 lb., for sale.

* In 1564, there was an individual connected with Dysart of the name of George Hakat, who is termed "commissionar of scotts privaleges in flandaris," but who at this time made his will, being in a state of bad health.

These rods were attempted to be introduced into this town and neighbourhood; but the nail-makers almost unanimously rejected this innovation on their old-established practice. Very few could be found to make use of the rods. But while the old material was unquestionably superior to the new, yet the preparing of it took up a great deal of time and labour, and required, in a part of the process, the services of two individuals —one with the forehammer, (a heavy hammer, with a long handle, and which required both hands to wield,) and the other with the ordinary nail-making hammer. On the contrary, the rods were quite ready for making the nails out of, and a far greater number could be made by this new system, and could be brought into the market at a considerably lower rate than by the old process; and as the nail-makers here refused to change their old habits, the trade, consequently, went elsewhere. Besides, as their earnings had for a long time remained stationary, never, we believe, being more than a shilling a day, while the wages of all other workmen had been gradually rising—and be it kept in mind that the price of the necessaries of life was also rising in an equal ratio—by the end of the last century none of the young lads in the district were sent to learn the making of nails, but went to learn other trades. Yea, we have known sons of nailers, who were taught to make nails when they were mere boys, when they grew up, forsook this occupation, and went to others. Thus the old nailers died out, and there were no young ones to fill up the broken ranks. These circumstances account for the total annihilation of the nail-making trade in this town.

The nail-makers had a very prosperous benefit society

in this town for many years, but the number of members lessened as the trade declined ; and, in the year
1805 or 1806, their numbers had dwindled down to
fourteen or fifteen, besides a few widows ; so the society
was broken up—their heritable property, which was
considerable, sold, and the proceeds divided.

The weaving trade now demands our consideration.
It is certain that there were weavers in this neighbourhood one hundred and fifty years ago ; how many,
or what proportion they bore to the entire population,
we have no means of ascertaining. We are equally
ignorant of the amount of the wages that they earned
at the beginning of last century. We have no reason,
however, for supposing that their earnings were greater
than that of other mechanics. Their number, however,
increased so much during the century, that, at the end
of it, they formed the most numerous class of the community. We have no separate account of the quantity
of cloth manufactured in this town during last century,
but statements have been preserved regarding the increasing prosperity of *the district* in this respect. In
1737, there were 177,740 yards of linen manufactured
in the district of Kirkcaldy. In 1743, 316,550 yards ;
value, £11,000. In 1755, the estimated value was
£22,000. In 1773, the value had decreased to £15,000,
in consequence of the interruption of foreign wars ;
but, however, the manufacturers of this district began
to prepare goods for the English market, and the trade
increased considerably in consequence. In 1792, it is
said, that taking in Largo on the east, and Leslie on
the north, there were 810 looms at work. In 1830,
there were 2000 looms in the parish of Dysart. It
is supposed that, at the present moment, the value of
goods manufactured in the same extended district is

not less than £200,000 annual value. In former days, and even in our own recollection, the manufacturers bought their own flax, gave it out to be spun, bleached and dyed it themselves; but in these days of division of labour, this practice has entirely ceased.

During the last decade of the eighteenth century, there were several streets built in this town and neighbourhood, exclusively for weavers' shops, and for dwelling-houses for their families. Their wages appear to have risen gradually from 1793, or perhaps sooner, until 1800, when coarse tikes—three leaves, we mean, of thirty-one porters and under—were 2s. 1d. per spindle; but from 1804, or earlier, until May 1808, the same work stood at 2s. 7d., at which period what is technically termed the *blue rod* was introduced; that is, dressing each colour of yarn separately. This produced, virtually, a fall of wages; but the impression on our mind is, that the highest wages ever paid in this locality for weaving was in 1815; but in the following year they fell very low; for there was a general stagnation of trade, so that webs could not be procured even at the low wages; and, to add to the calamity, the harvest of 1816 was the worst that had been seen since 1799—so that weavers were subjected to very great privations in consequence. There have been, of course, various fluctuations, more or less, in the rate of wages, and in the supply of webs, since that period, but the number of weavers has very much fallen off within the last ten years, in consequence of steam factories having been established in this neighbourhood; and there can be little doubt that, in a few years more, handloom weaving will be numbered with the things that were. But, in connexion with this, it should be noted that a considerable number of females find employment in the factories and spinning-mills in the vicinity; a number of men are also employed at the same works in various ways, and at other public works; so that it may be said that, upon the whole, there is as much employment now for male and female as there was forty or fifty years ago; although it should be borne in mind that, while in this neighbourhood the wages of several classes of workmen have of late years risen, the wages of weavers have fallen considerably, being lower now than they were in 1800. It is a great mercy that the changes which have taken place in regard to employment for the working classes have taken place gradually. The weavers pushed the nailers out of existence, and now the mills and factories are pushing the weavers out of sight. This is a changeable world in which we live.

In close connexion with the remarks which we have just been making, we cannot avoid noticing a very general and profitable employment in which females were engaged last century, and, indeed, centuries before, but which is now wholly laid aside. We refer to spinning. We can recollect the time when the spinning-wheel was to be seen in every house. Before spinning-mills were invented, the spinning-wheel was indispensable to the very existence of the weaver trade, and it was indispensable to the comfort of many a poor man's family. It was the means of eking out the scanty earnings of the nail-makers, the out-door labourers, and, indeed, as we have said, it was found in every house in this locality—not merely in the houses of the humble classes, but also in the houses of the well-to-do kind of people, even of those who kept servants. To explain this, it must be noted, that every family in those days, whether

rich or poor, spun their own linen, sheets, towelling,
&c.   All this ceaseless and universal birring of wheels
at the fireside has vanished, like the baseless fabric of
a vision.   The greater part of the females who were
thus employed have been under the necessity of going
out of doors to earn a livelihood, at the handloom, the
factory, the bleachfield, &c.   All the changes we have
noticed in regard to weaving, and other occupations
connected with it, have, in the first place, come about
gradually, as we have already said; but, in the second
place, some of those changes were indispensable.  Spin-
ning-wheels could not supply the twentieth part of the
yarn required now by the factories, and the handlooms
which are still in operation.

The wages of masons in the early part of last century, varied from 13⅓d. to 15d. per day; thatchers,
10d. to 10½d. per day; common labourers, 8d. per
day; and thatchers' service-men, 6⅔d. per day.   In
1756, thatchers were paid 13⅓d. per day, and their
service-men 8d. per day.   In 1802, masons' wages
had risen to 2s. 4d. per day, and their labourers to
1s. 4d. per day.

Previous to this century, the brewers appear to have
been a very active and prosperous class; maltmen, as
they were generally termed.   We can at the present moment point out at least fifteen places in this town where
ale was brewed for the use of the thirsty inhabitants.
We do not assert that all these were in actual operation at the same time, but, no doubt, the greater part
of them were.   The price of the article does not appear
to have varied for more than a hundred years—namely,
one penny the choppin.   In the beginning of this century, when there were still four or five brewers in the
town, the writer often went to one of them with a

"*pint stoup*" for three mutchkins, price 1½d. Of course, there was another kind of ale in use, double the strength of the ordinary kind, and double the price. When the breweries were in the height of their prosperity, tea as a daily beveridge was almost unknown to the working-classes in this locality. But notwithstanding the great increase of duty which the Government put on this article from time to time, it continued to force its way into general use, so that there is not now a family in this neighbourhood, we believe, which does not make use of it daily, less or more. Thus, as the use of tea increased, the use of ale and beer decreased, so that there is not now a single brewery in this town and neighbourhood. We conceive that this change of beverage has been productive of the most beneficial effects on the health and comfort of the community.

As intimately connected with the brewing of ale and beer, we may here say a few words about the sale of other intoxicating drinks. About the year 1800, there were about nine or ten houses in the town licensed for the manufacture or sale of strong drink, when the population was little more than half of what it is at present. But a very rapid increase took place in the number of public-houses during the first quarter of this century. In the year 1822, the Government made a great reduction in the duty on home-made spirits. We do not pretend to say that this was the *sole* cause of the unprecedented increase of places where intoxicants were sold; but it is a certain fact, that in the year 1829, there were twenty-six houses licensed to sell spirits, porter, and ale, in the town of Pathhead, exclusive of St Clairtown. In 1830, there were twenty-five. A temperance society was established in this town in the

last named year, and the number of licensed houses
fell off gradually, until three or four years ago they
were reduced to six, but now they have increased to
nine in number, and that is just about the number
which existed in 1800.

From time immemorial there have always been a
number of seafaring men belonging to this place. The
town of Pathhead being situated in the vicinity of two
seaports, it is no great wonder to see young lads, who
may be wishing for a change of employment, or who
may be desirous of seeing the world, bid farewell to
the workshop, and take up with the sea as their future
occupation. It is worthy of remark, that in very few
instances indeed, does any youth leave this neighbourhood, and go to sea, without having been for some
time, at least, learning some trade. This circumstance
is productive of the most beneficial consequences to
such in after years. While seafaring men at the principal seaports in England and Scotland have very little
employment in winter, those belonging to this place
are generally employed at the trade which they learned
in their youth. But moreover, many of them, after
having been at sea for a number of years, leave it off
altogether, and settle at home.

---

## GENERAL HISTORY OF PATHHEAD.

It will be perceived that we have thrown a considerable portion of historical matter connected with Pathhead into separate sections, a plan which we conceive
will be generally approved of by our readers as tending to make the whole work more clear and intelligible.
Of course, this will render this part of the work more

brief and easy. With all the diligent search which we
have made, we have not been able to ascertain the
exact period when the town of Pathhead began to
exist. We know, indeed, that the *estate* of Dunnikier
existed as a distinct property as far back as September
9, 1513, when the battle of Flodden was fought; but
whether there had been any feus granted by the proprietors at that time, we cannot tell. Of this we are
certain, that in the year 1582, David Lundie of Bal-
gonie, the then superior of Dunnikier, granted feus;
how many we do not know, and we are equally ignorant whether these were the first or not. At this period
Scotland was just emerging from the darkness of
Popery. The parish of Dysart had been pre-eminently
the seat of the beast, on a small scale. As far as we
can see, there was not a place in the whole county of
Fife with the same population, where there were so
many popish priests. There could not be fewer than
six or seven, while the population was under 2000.
There was a rector, a vicar, and it is supposed that
there were priests who officiated at the altars of St
James, St John, Trinity, and the cell of St Catherine—
all in the church; besides the chapel of St Dennis, and
also the cave of St Serf. All these priests had to be
fed and clad; their mistresses, and their illegitimate
offspring, had to be fed and clad also. They had a
slice off every loaf. The poor man's upper claith at
death, and the rich man's acres at all times, were
eagerly appropriated by them. A very great amount
of land was in the possession of the Church, *alias* the
clergy, at the time of the Reformation. It may appear
a perfect mystery to some, how it came about that such
a nest of owls were located in Dysart. The only way
by which we can account for it, is this: Dysart, al-

though a small place, considered in itself, was of very great importance, as being the centre of a large portion of the county of Fife, for the transactions of civil matters. Individuals residing as far west as Aberdour, as far north as Leslie, and as far east as Pittenweem, resorted to Dysart for the purpose of making transferences of property. *A great many of these transactions took place in the church.* The town-clerk's office in Dysart must have been a very lucrative one in those days. And we may be sure that the priests would be always on the look-out to obtain some nice pickings for the Church, or for themselves, which was the same thing. Thus previous to the Reformation, "darkness covered the earth, and gross darkness the people," and to no part of the country of Scotland could this language be applied with more propriety than to the parish of Dysart, including our own little village.

The Parliament of Scotland assembled on Monday the 12th March 1543. The whole of the business that came before them was transacted on Tuesday, Wednesday, and Thursday, although it was Saturday before it formally broke up. On Thursday, the 15th, a bill was presented by Lord Maxwell, for allowing the Scriptures to be read by all without limitation, and the Lords of the Articles found, because there was no law shewn or produced to the contrary, that the same may be used by *all the lieges of this realm in our vulgar tongue ;* and therefore, in full Parliament, allowed the bill to be read. Dunbar, who was Archbishop of Glasgow, and also Lord Chancellor, rose up, and " in his own name, and in the name of *all* the prelates of the realm that were present, dissented *simpliciter.*" The whole of the clergy present followed his example, opposing the passing of such an Act, and proposing

that it should be postponed, at least, until the whole
clergy of Scotland should have an opportunity of de-
liberating on the matter. But the opposition of the
clergy, in the Parliament, was in vain. They were
weakened considerably by the absence of the primate,
Archbishop Beaton, who was at this time a prisoner in
St Andrews, he having rendered himself obnoxious to
the Queen Regent and the Earl of Arran, for having
forged a will, purporting to be the will of the late
James V., constituting him guardian of the infant Queen
Mary, and governor of the kingdom of Scotland.

The bill passed into a law in these terms:—" It is
statute and ordained that it shall be lawful to *all our
Sovereign Lady's lieges to have the holy writ, both of the
Old and the New Testament, in the vulgar tongue, in the
English or Scottish, of a good and true translation, and
that they shall incur no crimes for the having or reading
of the same, providing always, that no man dispute or
hold opinions, under the pains contained in* " " the Acts
of Parliament."

On Monday the 19th, public proclamation was made
of the new law at the market-cross of Edinburgh, also
in Dundee, Aberdeen, Elgin, Forres, Inverness, Dunfermline, Perth, Lanark, Dumfries, Kirkcudbright, and
Wigtown.

This Parliament is described as being *the most substantial Parliament that ever was seen in man's remembrance.* And what was very remarkable, and clearly
shews the special interposition of the Supreme Ruler of
the universe in behalf of His own cause, that Act of
Parliament was never repealed. Although the agents
of the great whore had it in their power, for a number
of years after this, to molest and persecute to the
death many of the lovers of the Bible; yet there this

Act stood firm, granting power to *all* to read. and consequently to procure for themselves the sacred volume. And, be it remarked, that copies of the Scriptures had, for the previous sixteen years, been smuggled into Scotland from the Continent.    John Knox says of this year :—" *Then might have been seen the Bible lying upon almost every gentleman's table    The New Testament was borne about in many men's hands.*"

On Sunday, the 3d of September, the Earl of Arran, the governor of Scotland, who gave his sanction to the passing of the Act, went from Stirling to Callander House to meet the primate, Archbishop Beaton, and threw himself into his arms, abjuring his new idea in favour of " the old learning ; " and from the man he had imprisoned in January received absolution in September for all that he had done.    Nevertheless, neither the primate nor the governor ever had the power, although they had the will, to rescind the Act of Parliament that set the Bible free.

But now the light began to break in upon the darkness.    Copies of the Holy Scriptures, of Tindal's translation, began to be imported into England and Scotland from Holland and Flanders.    Although such importation was sternly prohibited in this country, yet Bibles and Testaments were being brought safely from the Continent in almost every bale of goods, and they were eagerly read by all who could lay their hands on them.    This was a far more valuable importation to the community than old iron, Dutch presses, or Delft ware.    There is a remarkable circumstance mentioned by Christopher Anderson in his Annals of the English Bible, in connexion with this.    The Parliament of Scotland met at Edinburgh, at a time when Beaton, then only Archbishop, was absent, and under a cloud.

A certain lord, (I have forgot his name), brought forward a motion to this effect, that every person in the kingdom should be permitted to read the Bible who thought proper to do so. The clergy, with the Archbishop of Glasgow at their head, of course opposed the motion; but Beaton being absent, their opposition was ineffectual, for the whole of the lay members voted for it. This permission to read virtually implied permission to purchase the Word of God. There were two circumstances, very remarkable and worthy of our notice, in connexion with this permission to read the Bible. *First,* When this new Act of Parliament became known, it was found that there was a copy of the Scriptures in almost every person's possession that was able to purchase one. And *second,* although immediately after the Act had passed, Beaton emerged from his confinement, and the regent in a most cowardly manner went to meet him, and recanted his Protestant errors, and obtained absolution, yet this Act of Parliament was never repealed. We may rest assured that the inhabitants of this district would not be behind hand in taking advantage, *first,* of their facilities for procuring copies of the Scriptures from the Continent; and *second,* in openly reading them when they had legal permission to do so. There can be no doubt that the seaports on the south coast of Fife would have their full share of this item of trade. Thus the darkness of Popery was dispelled. Let it never be forgotten that it was the *people* who carried on the Reformation in Scotland in spite of the Government, and not, as in England, where it was *vice versa* The church in Dysart was denuded of its priest and altars, and *red* and fitted up, although imperfectly, for Protestant worship.*

* Just about the time of the Reformation, namely, in 1562, in

For a hundred years after the commencement of the Reformation we have little to chronicle concerning Pathhead. Whatever time it may have begun to appear as a town, we know from good authority that in 1666 there were eighty houses in it. The estate had passed through a number of hands; but, notwithstanding, the feuars had evidently been increasing in numbers. In that year, John Watson, sen., went to law with the feuars for the purpose of depriving them of their privilege of taking stones and clay, fail and divet, from the whole Muir of Dunnikier, which they had enjoyed since the year 1608; but as we have referred particularly to this matter in our section on the Farm, it is unnecessary to say anything on it here. In 1637, in Dysart, it was enjoined, " the browsters to brew guid and sufficient ail for sixtein pennies the pynt—weill leavened white bread of fourteine uncis wecht for twelf pennys—guid and sufficient quhyt candile best mixture or craking, fourtie pennys the pund—the ait to be tasted by men of skill." The price, in Fife, of bear was £10; of aits and meal, £19. No other prices in the fiars at that time.

The inhabitants of the parishes of Dysart and Kirkcaldy took an active part in the religious and civil transactions of the middle portion of the seventeenth century. It has been said that ninety of the inhabitants of Dysart fell in one battle that was fought during that period of turmoil,[*] and two hundred widows were also

Dysart, the price of " quhyt was three pund the boll; boll of beir fourtie twa schillingis." The price was considerably more than double a hundred years afterwards.

* The years 1649, 1650, 1651, and 1652, were very trying years for Scotland in general, and for Fife in particular. The price of grain in those years rose to above double what they were the previous years. Wheat £16 and £17 per boll; oatmeal £16 per boll. This was in Fife, while on the south side of the

said to have been made in Kirkcaldy on the same occasion; but we would fain think that this was an exaggerated statement. The inhabitants of Pathhead' were, of course, mixed up with the one town or the other, or both, in their labours and sufferings. The same remark may also be made regarding the swearing of the covenants in this neighbourhood. All, it is said, attended to that ceremony. There were no dissenters in those days. Indeed, none were tolerated. The principles of civil and religious liberty were then but very imperfectly understood. Every one seemed to understand what his *own* rights were, but very few appeared to understand what rights his neighbour ought to enjoy. This one-sided view of the subject led to much confusion and much suffering during the greater part of the seventeenth century. However, since the happy change of matters which took place at the revolution of 1688, light has been gradually breaking in upon men's minds on this very important point; men are beginning to understand more practically than ever, our Lord's golden rule, "Whatsoever ye would that men should do to you, do ye even so to them, for this is the law and the prophets."

Forth prices were still higher. Cheese was £3 per stone, and butter £6 per stone. In the first of these years, the spring was cold and dry and late, and in harvest there were great rains; and plenty of snow fell also. There were other causes than the bad seasons which tended to make provisions dear. Scotland was invaded by Cromwell, and constant levies were made of horse and foot for the defence of the country. Fife was particularly oppressed. In February 1651, two regiments of horse and two of foot were levied in the county; that was the fourth levy in twelve months. In the same year there were twelve regiments of horse and five of foot quartered within its bounds. In 1653 there was a plentiful harvest, and prices fell to one-half of what they had been for the preceding four years.

In 1684 John Watson, sen., gave the first piece of
burying-ground for the use of the haill inhabitants of
Dunnikier, and in 1707 they assessed themselves for
the purpose of enclosing it, as noted in another part of
our work.    In 169—, John Watson, jun., received the
first *royal charter* for the estate of Dunnikier, it being
granted by Queen Anne, (commonly called Anne of
Denmark,) with consent of James VI., her husband;
and in July 1695 the same gentleman obtained an Act
of Parliament, authorising the holding of two annual
fairs in the town, to continue three days each.

In the year 1736 an event happened in Scotland, in
which the town of Pathhead was specially interested,
and which made a great noise in the whole country for
a considerable time; we refer to the Porteous Riot.
Every historian who has gone over the history of the
period in which it happened has taken notice of it.
We shall endeavour to give the particulars of this
strange affair as briefly as possible.    Andrew Wilson
was a native of Pathhead, a baker by trade, son of
Alexander Wilson, baker also, there, but who had died
about three years previous to the commencement of
our story.    Andrew had been engaged in a number of
smuggling transactions in this neighbourhood.    He was
a heavy, powerful man, and, withal, very daring and
reckless.    The officers of excise or customs had on
several occasions made seizures of smuggled goods from
him, which irritated him very much.    He therefore
determined that he would obtain satisfaction for the
losses which he had sustained; if he could not get
back the identical goods which had been taken from
him, he would attack some of the Government officials,
and take from them what he considered to be an equi-
valent in money.    Accordingly, when in Edinburgh,

(whether he went there for that purpose or not, does not appear,) he entered into a combination with George Robertson, who kept an inn at Bristo, and William Hall, also an inhabitant of Edinburgh, to waylay Mr James Stark, the collector of excise in Kirkcaldy, while on his round collecting in the eastern part of the county of Fife. And, moreover, it is asserted that Wilson formed the design of thus robbing Mr Stark several months previous. Accordingly, on the 9th of January, William Hall having come across the Firth from Edinburgh, he hired two horses from Patrick Galloway, horse-hirer in Kinghorn, and took with him John Galloway, a son or servant of Patrick Galloway— Wilson and Robertson, who, it appears, were in another house, having also horses engaged, going by themselves, and Hall and Galloway by themselves. The two latter named individuals reached Anstruther Easter about six o'clock in the evening, and put up their horses at a James Wilson's there, where they found Wilson already there before them ; but the whole four were together, shortly after, in Anstruther. Between ten and eleven o'clock, the whole four went on foot to Pittenweem, to the house of Mrs Fowler, where Mr Stark was lodging for the night, who had a room for himself, William Geddes, his clerk, being in a room next his, along with Alexander Clerk, supervisor of excise in Cupar.

All the three retired to their respective bed-rooms at ten o'clock, but about an hour and a-half afterwards were awakened by a violent knocking at the collector's door. This knocking appears to have been by Andrew Wilson, who beat in the lower part of the door ; but before he had been able to effect an entrance, the collector had jumped out of the window in his shirt, two storeys high, taking with him a bag of money, leaving behind him a purse with fifty-two guineas, and six or seven pounds of silver in it, as also a pocket-book, containing £41 in bank-notes.   While Wilson was committing the robbery, Robertson was standing sentry at the door, with a drawn cutlass in his hand, to prevent any person from entering.   Of course the noise and disturbance in the house was very great : the robbers cursing and swearing, and the landlady and servants weeping and lamenting.   After taking this money that the collector had left, and several other articles belonging to him, which they secured about their persons or threw away at different places, they left the house; but Mr Clerk having gone in great haste to Anstruther, and obtained the assistance of a sergeant and a few privates, in a few hours the criminals were apprehended, and not very long afterwards all the stolen property was recovered.

Wilson, Robertson, and Hall were carried to Edinburgh, and were tried by the High Court of Justiciary, Duncan Forbes, Esq., who was afterwards Lord President of the Court of Session, being at the time Lord Advocate.   All three were found guilty, and were sentenced to be executed in the Grassmarket of Edinburgh, on the 14th of April.   What became of Hall we have never learned ; but his sentence must have been commuted.   The other two prisoners were left for execution.

There are some rather out of the way circumstances connected with this case : First, on the side of the prosecution.   In the indictment Wilson was charged with having *formed the design* of robbing Mr Stark, and, of course, that this was the object he had in view in going to Anstruther and Pittenweem.   But there was not a single witness brought forward at the trial in order to prove that the robbery was premeditated. And further, it is remarkable that Mrs Fowler, the landlady of the house wherein the collector was robbed, and who was in conversation with both Wilson and Robertson immediately before the robbery was committed, was not brought forward as a witness on the trial, although her servant-man and servant-maid both were. On the other hand, the panels did not bring forward a single witness in defence. Their counsel, indeed, alleged in defence that Wilson and Robertson, instead of going from Edinburgh to Anstruther for the purpose of robbing the collector, were going on lawful business, namely, to purchase brandy, and that in order to effect that object, they were provided with a letter of credit from Francis Russel, druggist, directed to Bailie Waddel, Cellardyke, and also an accepted bill of John Fullarton, Causeyside, to the same amount, yet no evidence was brought forward to prove the truth of these assertions. John Galloway, indeed, who was retained as a witness for the prosecution, deponed that Hall told him at Kinghorn that they were going to Anstruther to get some brandy, and that Wilson and Robertson were to be their paymasters. The panels further alleged that they were under the influence of strong drink when the robbery was committed; and we frankly admit that the conduct of Wilson and Robertson —the former, in making a noise in breaking up a door sufficient to waken up not only all the inmates of the house, but also many of the surrounding inhabitants; and the latter, in standing sentry at the door of the house with a drawn cutlass in his hand—was more like that of persons drunk or mad than of sober or sane persons. But the robbery itself was clearly proved by evidence, and was never denied by the prisoners, and that was a penal offence at that period. With these remarks we drop the subject.

Such a sentence was by no means in accordance with the view which many of the inhabitants of Scotland entertained regarding the practice of smuggling; and it has always been found that when a sentence has been unusually severe, or too severe for the punishment of the crime of which a prisoner is found guilty, hatred of the crime is changed into sympathy with the criminal. Of course these individuals had been guilty of housebreaking, and the law at that time, and until very lately, treated that crime as a capital one. But, notwithstanding, a very general sympathy was manifested for the two individuals. There were confined in the room immediately above them two horse-stealers, (horse-stealing was also a capital crime then,) named Ratcliff and Stewart, who had been brought from Arbroath some time before this, having procured from their friends spring-saws, &c., sawed through the bars of their windows; they then made a hole in the floor, and pulled up through it Wilson and Robertson. Stewart got out safe from the window by means of a rope. Wilson made the attempt next, but being a bulky individual, stuck fast in the window, and before any of the rest could make their escape, they were discovered and better secured. This was on a Friday morning, and the execution of Wilson and Robertson was appointed to take place on the Wednesday following. On Sabbath the 11th, the two prisoners were taken to the Tolbooth Church to hear the condemned sermon, as it was termed, according to custom, guarded by four soldiers. While the people were coming into the church, Wilson attempted to make his escape, but finding that impracticable, he seized hold of three of the soldiers, one with each hand and another with his teeth, and cried out, "Geordie, do for your life." Geordie of course sprang out of the seat, knocked over the fourth soldier, ran over the tops of the pews with incredible agility, the audience opening a way sufficient to receive them both, and in hurrying out at the south gate he tumbled over the plate with the collection. He got clear off, while Wilson was immediately taken back to the jail, and on the day appointed was executed in the Grassmarket. He was interred in Pathhead burying-ground.

The conduct of Andrew Wilson, in thus assisting so manfully the escape of his fellow-prisoner, when he had not the faintest ray of hope of his own deliverance, drew forth the sympathy of thousands, not only in Edinburgh but in all parts of the country where the circumstances were known. The magistrates, being aware of this feeling, took every precaution that they could think of to prevent a rescue. They locked the executioner up in the tolbooth, lest he might have been taken out of the way on the day of execution; the sentries were doubled on the outside of the jail, besides those posted within; the officers of the trained bands were ordered to attend the execution; also the constables, with long batons; the whole city guard had ammunition distributed to them, and marched to the place of execution with fixed bayonets, intermixed with the town-officers; and to make the work quite sure, a detachment of the Welsh Fusileers drew up on each side of the Lawnmarket, while another detachment stood under arms at the Canongate guard. The execution, however, passed off as quietly as on other occasions,—there was not the least appearance of any desire on the part of any of the spectators to rescue the unfortunate man from his fate. When life was extinct, the magistrates retired to a house hard by, rightly supposing that all fear of any tumult was at an end. However, when the hangman went on the ladder to cut down the body, some idle boys began to throw pebbles or garbage at him. This so enraged Captain Porteous, who commanded the city guard, and who, it was said, was inflamed with drink at the time, that, without any orders from the magistrates, or reading the Riot Act, he commanded the guards to fire,— which they were quite unwilling to do ;—and it is even said that he seized hold of a musket from one of his men and fired it himself. Several individuals were killed, and a number more wounded, some very dangerously.

The magistrates, after ordering the dead to be buried and the wounded looked after at their expense, immediately convened in council, and, after taking a precognition of the circumstances, ordered Captain Porteous to be apprehended and put in jail. The conduct of Captain Porteous on this occasion drew forth a universal burst of indignation from the inhabitants of Scotland, who called upon the authorities to bring him to trial for murder. The Government felt itself compelled to yield to this universal cry, and Porteous was tried and found guilty, and sentenced to be executed on the 8th of September 1736.

However, the Government, considering that there were some extenuating circumstances in the case, sent down to Edinburgh a six weeks' reprieve for the culprit. This act was interpreted by the public as merely a prelude to the granting of a free pardon. In consequence of this, a number of individuals banded themselves together, and determined that they would take the law into their own hands, and hang him themselves. A plan was secretly concocted that completely baffled the authorities. Where or by whom this plan was originated, has never to this day been discovered. But the plan *was* laid, and completely succeeded. On the Tuesday evening, (the day before the execution was to have taken place,) a number of individuals seized the drum belonging to the suburb of Portsburgh, and, pressing the drummer's son into the service, they shut all the gates of the city to prevent the soldiers, who were quartered in the Canongate, or any other parties, from interfering in the execution of their plan; a mob was collected by beat of drum; they went to the guard-house and disarmed the sentries, seized all the arms that were there, and then proceeded to the prison, the door of which they attempted to break open; but it resisting all their endeavours, they brought fire to bear upon it, which in course of time took effect; and thus obtaining an entrance, they forced the keys from the keepers, and seizing Porteous, they hurried him out and carried him to the Grassmarket, where they hanged him on a dyer's pole. In order to obtain a piece of rope to execute their purpose, they broke into a shop and took as much as they wanted, and left the payment on the table. Having effected their purpose, they threw all the arms away which they had taken from the guard-house, and instantly dispersed,—and the body hung until next morning. A reward of £200 was offered to any one who would discover the leaders of this extraordinary project. But the most remarkable circumstance connected with this transaction remains to be told—namely, that notwithstanding the offer of so large a reward, no reliable information regarding the origin of this outrage, or the names of the leaders, ever reached the ears of the Government. A number of persons were examined, and one individual was tried, but all came to nothing. It is asserted by historians that there were people present upon the occasion from the counties of Fife, Stirling, East Lothian, Dumfries; and, Andrew Wilson belonging to Pathhead, the people took a deep interest in the matter. A number of young lads went from the town, and were present at the execution of Porteous. One of them, of whom we have a distinct recollection, went with a companion round by the Bridge of Stirling, dressed in women's clothes. But what part any of our townsmen took in this extraordinary affair we have never learned. The British Parliament took up the matter warmly, and sent for the magistrates of Edinburgh and the judges, and a proclamation was drawn up which all the ministers of the Established Church of Scotland were required to read every Sabbath for a twelvemonth; but, as we have already observed, no evidence was ever obtained that could implicate any individual.

On the 7th January 1740, being Handsell Monday, a very melancholy accident happened in this neighbourhood. A number of boys were playing in a cove on the south side of the town, when a large mass of rock fell upon them, by which ten of them were crushed to death. Their names were as follows—viz., William Miller, son of James Miller, elder, weaver; Henry and James Whyte, sons of David Whyte, maltster; Henry Scott, son of Thomas Scott, shoemaker; Robert Ross, son of James Ross, hammerman; John and Andrew Mairns, sons of John Mairns, hammerman; James Alison, son of Thomas Alison, candlemaker; Alexander Anderson, son of the deceased James Anderson, hammerman; and Andrew Hay, son of the deceased George Hay, tailor in the Milltown. Such a catastrophe happening in a small village, as Pathhead was at that time, would not soon be forgotten. It spread lamentation and woe, not only in the families of those who suffered, but through the whole community.

This unfortunate cove was situated a few yards west from the foot of the Vennel. In the early part of this century there was still a slight recess in the rock at the spot where the cove once existed; but the rock being freestone, it has been quarried and carried away for building purposes, so that not a vestige remains now of the place where so many of the young inhabitants of this town came to their untimely end.

In this same year, a scarcity of food was felt in this place, occasioned by a deficiency of crop. Such deficiencies, indeed, happened very frequently in Scotland, and in other countries too, in bygone times; and much privation and suffering was the consequence. For although it has scarcely ever happened that the crops have failed in every country on the face of the globe in the same year, yet there were no facilities then as now for bringing the surplus of food which might be in any country to the relief of another, which might be suffering from famine. There were no corn merchants or agents in those days to gather up the superabundant food in any district, in order to supply the wants of another district in a distant part of the world. There was an equal scarcity of shipping for carrying the surplus food, if it *had been gathered* together. Thus, as we have said, when a scarcity of food existed in any country, the relief which it obtained from another was but trifling, and much suffering was experienced by the people in consequence. In 1700, and the previous six years, commonly termed the seven dear years, such a failure of the crop occurred in Scotland, that many persons died for want on the highways. "During this period, great scarcity prevailed all over Scotland, approaching to a famine, and accumulated every year, till at last the absolute necessaries of life could scarcely be got for money in the most fertile districts. Inferior barleymeal sold for a merk the peck, while oatmeal was not to be purchased. Greens boiled in salt became a common food in various places. Pestilence succeeded the famine. Moreover, fodder was as scarce as grain—many of the cattle dying at the stall. The country was drained and impoverished by large sums exported for grain. The causes of the scarcity were, that the harvests were late, and the winters early, so that the frost and snow blasted the growing corns." But the year 1740, was indeed a year of great calamity to all the inhabitants of Scotland. On the night of June 13, one of the most tremendous hurricanes, accompanied with lightning, commenced, such as had not been known for a long time in this country; the lead roofs of the buildings in Edinburgh castle were rolled up and blown over the walls, and in the Parliament House, about twelve hundredweight was carried into the midst of the square. Throughout the country, the damage was immense; corns were scattered about the fields, and great numbers of cattle perished in the ruins of their stables, &c. &c.; the shores were strewed with wrecks, and many people perished. An intense frost had set in on Christmas day, which lasted until the end of February. The Forth was intensely frozen over above Alloa, the mills were everywhere stopped, and a great dearth succeeded; oatmeal rose to the price of two shillings sterling the peck, and at one time could hardly be procured for money; the depth of snow prevented coals being carried to any distance, so that many of the poor perished with cold. No doubt, the inhabitants of this place had their share of this calamity. We think that it is very plainly implied in what we are now going to record, that there was a scarcity of food, and the authorities at least *suspected* that there were certain parties in the neighbourhood, who were wishing to fish in troubled waters, for their own advantage, no doubt. In October that year, there was a Head Court held in reference to this matter. A complaint had been lodged with the Bailie, " that several dissolute and disorderly people had for some days past banded themselves together, under pretence of meal being concealed in some houses, with threatenings to search the said houses where they suspected such meal lay." However, inquiry having been made, the conclusion had been come to by the Bailie, that there was no ground for supposing that there was any unreasonable quantity of meal hoarded up in the town; and in order that the peace might be preserved, no fewer than twenty-six individuals from all the different quarters of the town were appointed, and instructed to warn all the householders in their respective localities, against themselves, or children, or apprentices giving any assistance to the disorderly persons referred to, and even to keep themselves in readiness to oppose any attack if it were made ; but at the same time it was ordained, that if, upon inquiry, it was found that any quantity of meal was hoarded up, more than was sufficient for the ordinary course of sale, complaint was to be made to the Bailie, who would cause it to be brought out and sold at the current prices.

We now come down to the " '45," a very remark-

able year in Scottish history.    A party of Charles' ad-
herents passed through this town, and the news of their
approach caused considerable excitement among the
inhabitants.    There was perhaps little cause for alarm
as regards their leaders, for they paid, we believe, for
what supplies they obtained in the neighbourhood.    It
is not yet many years since the individuals passed
away from this scene who drove hay and straw from
Sauchenbuss to their quarters; but although the officials whose duty it was to obtain such articles for the
troops under their command might be strictly honourable in their dealings, yet the inhabitants of this place
could not have forgotten the tales which their grandfathers had told them about the excesses of " the High-
land host " during the troublous times in the preceding
century.    They were not *very sure*, therefore, but that
some of the Highlanders in Charlie's army might make
more free than welcome with any little thing that
might suit them, unknown to their officers.    Thus we
are informed that when it was rumoured that the rebels
were drawing near to this neighbourhood, those who
had ponies contrived to take them to a place of con-
cealment where no stranger would ever think of looking
for them.    This was the spacious garret belonging now
to Mr John Thomson, at the west end of Nether Street.
There is still shewn the steps which were broken by
the hoofs of the animals in their ascent to their hiding-
place.    And we believe instances occurred of individuals
secreting articles of value on the rumoured approach of
the rebels, but which they never were able to lay their
hands on again.    An instance of this occurred to a
certain young man, (we did not learn his name,) a servant to Mr William Whyte, farmer and maltster, who,
having a few bank-notes, which he wished to preserve

from the clutches of the rebels, went and hid them safely, as he imagined, in the hole of a dyke somewhere at the back of the town, but some other person had appropriated them to his own use. But that individuals in the rebel army actually did work for their own hand when it could conveniently be done, the following anecdote will shew:—One of the Highlanders, in coming along on the march in the neighbourhood of this town, happening to see a young man standing at the roadside with a pair of good shoes on his feet, on which he cast a wistful eye, and accordingly gave him a gentle hint that he wished to make an exchange with him. The lad, however, not thinking that this would be a *fair* exchange, exclaimed, " I am one of Charlie's men." But the Highlander immediately retorted, " I dinna care whether you be ane o' Sharlie's men or Shordie's men, but your brogues pe petter than mine;" so a forced exchange of shoes had to be submitted to.

Every person in this neighbourhood must have heard of Paul Jones appearing in the Firth of Forth during the period of the American revolutionary war. He was a native of the west of Scotland; had been at sea in his youth, but afterwards settled in America. The revolutionary war called him out from his retirement, and he entered into the naval service of his adopted country. It is said that he was the first individual who hoisted the thirteen stars and stripes on board of a vessel of war. He was entrusted with the command of two or three vessels, and made a descent upon his native coast in the west of Scotland. After a hard-fought action, he captured the *Serapis*, a British 44-gun ship as she was convoying a fleet of merchant-menfrom the Baltic to this country. (This vessel was afterwards retaken, we do not know by whom, but we

have seen her.)   In consequence of such deeds his
name spread terror along all the coasts of Great Britain.
In September 1779, he was seen making for the Firth
of Forth.   It appears that he was intending to land at
Leith, and levy a contribution of £200,000 from the
inhabitants—a princely sum, indeed, for such a place
as Leith then was.   He had a letter already written for sending ashore, and containing that extraordinary demand; and it was dated for the 17th of
that month, as expecting to be able to reach Leith
Roads by that time.   However, Divine Providence
frustrated his purposes, for after he was to the westward of Kirkcaldy, a gale of wind, or rather a hurricane,
drove him down the Firth on the 16th, the day previous
to that of his intended landing, and he never renewed
his attempt.

Mr Robert Shirra, the Burgher minister of Kirkcaldy,
has his name associated with this retreat of Paul Jones
in every narrative that has been given of it.   He lived
at the time in a part of that house which is now the
Post-office, and going down the garden and out at the
door at the foot of it, and there being no houses at that
period to intercept his view, he beheld the enemy endeavouring to work up the Firth.   A number of individuals were congregated there, watching the progress
of Paul.   It is a certain fact that Mr Shirra engaged
in prayer, but whether this was his own spontaneous
act, or that he was requested to do so by some of the
bystanders, is quite uncertain.   But it is a fact well
established, that while he was praying, or immediately
after, a furious gale arose, and compelled the intruder
to retrace his steps.

A native of Pathhead, now one of its oldest inhabitants, told us, a very short time ago, that on that

memorable day, being then a boy of four or five years
old, his father, who lived in that spot which is now
dignified with the name of Arthur's Neuk, took him
with him, as he was going to do some little job in a
garden which he had a lease of, and which was situated
a short distance east from his dwelling-house. On
their return home, his father having hold of his hand,
there came such a hurricane of wind along the Mid
Street from the western quarter, that his father was
quite unable to drag him along to the door of the
house, but was forced to take shelter at the gable,
where he stood with his back to the wall, firmly holding him by the hand all the while. It is somewhat
remarkable to obtain at the present moment such a
distinct corroboration of the tradition that a tremendous
gale drove away from our shores this formidable enemy,
Paul Jones.

The year 1794 was a rather remarkable one for the
inhabitants of Pathhead in two respects. It was in
this year that the first school-house in the locality was
built; and although this was an event that was the
beginning of a new era in the progress of education,
and was of immense importance to the rising generation, yet, as we have elsewhere recorded, it was productive of great anxiety and trouble to those who took an
active part in the bringing it about during the eight
years that it was under their management. This year
was also remarkable for the disease and mortality
which prevailed in the town. What exact amount
of disease there was among the inhabitants, we have
not been able to ascertain, but the number of deaths
was unprecedented, being no fewer than 97. In the
month of September they amounted to 19. This was
not a year of peculiar scarcity, the fiars' prices of the

year 1793 for oatmeal being 16s. 6d. per boll, and for 1794, 16s., so it was not famine that brought on this uncommon mortality, whatever might have been the cause.

About the year 1798, a circumstance occurred in Pathhead which disturbed for a little the equanimity of the inhabitants. My father was at that time mate of a vessel belonging to Shields, and she, requiring some repairs, was taken into a dry dock. My father embraced this opportunity to come home and visit his family. While crossing at Kinghorn Ferry, a conversation about political matters took place among the passengers. A certain worthy belonging to this place, who happened to be present, having heard my father make use of some expressions which he imagined bordered on sedition, as soon as he got home wrote a letter to a relation of his, who was an officer on board of a frigate then lying in Leith Roads, wherein he represented my father as a very dangerous character, and so forth. Immediately on this letter reaching its destination, a boat was dispatched from the frigate to Pettycur, with the crew well armed, who, as soon as they landed, proceeded to Pathhead for the purpose of seizing my father, and conveying him on board of the frigate. But ere they arrived, the bird was flown. My father had scarcely landed in his own house, when he received a letter summoning him to repair to his ship immediately, as she was already out of dock and preparing for sea, her damages not being so great as was anticipated. The frigate's boat's crew, after ascertaining that my father was out of their reach, were sauntering east the Nether Street, when they got sight of three or four young seafaring men conversing together. One of these young men, Andrew Wemyss by name, was standing near his father's door, when the boat's crew came up and laid hands on him, and dragged him away as fast as possible towards Pettycur, where their boat was lying. In the meantime, Andrew's companions fled in different directions, and got clear off. The news of his capture spread through the town, and a great number of people, both male and female, and armed with sticks or any other weapons, started in pursuit. The captive's father had mounted his cart-horse and rode off to Kinghorn, warning the people all the way as he went along about what had happened. The consequence was, that a great number of people collected, and surrounded the boat's crew at Kinghorn, and liberated the prisoner, whom they placed in a smith's shop, from whence he escaped by a back door, and went into the country. We have mentioned this circumstance in order to shew that, although natives of Pathhead have at all times been found in sufficient numbers in the army and navy, yet the idea of being *compelled* to enter such service has always been considered dreadfully oppressive. We do not here mean to assert that this feeling is peculiar to Pathhead, but it consists with our personal knowledge that it does exist here in an intense degree.

The dearth in 1799 and 1800 was a very trying state of things for the inhabitants of this place. Of course, the whole of the inhabitants of Scotland were suffering from the same cause, but that did not make the matter any better in this place. In 1797 the fiars' price of oatmeal was only 14s. 8d. per boll; for 1798 it was 15s. 6d.; but for 1799 it was £1, 12s.; while for 1800 it rose to the unprecedented figure of £2, 2s. In some instances it was retailed as high as 3s. 6d. per peck, but it even could not be procured at such a price.

People often travelled a number of miles to obtain it, and were frequently disappointed. Bearmeal, and it was very indifferent in quality, had often to be resorted to for the making of porridge, and people were glad to obtain even that. The writer can distinctly remember that when a lot of meal arrived at the Meal Society's store in Back Street, the outer door was barred, and only a few purchasers were permitted to enter at a time, and then at the spot where the meal was weighed there was a bar of wood fixed, outside of which *all* the buyers were kept, in order to prevent those who were engaged in weighing from being incommoded. The harvest of 1799 was a very bad one, and that of 1800 was not much better, and thus the food was brought up to famine price. However, it is worthy of being noticed that, exorbitant as was the price of grain, people did not suffer at this time as they had done in former years of scarcity, such as 1700 and 1740. In 1800 the wages of the greater portion of the working classes were double those of the former years; besides, there was plenty of work, especially in connexion with the manufacture of linen. Another circumstance deserves to be mentioned ;—in 1800 the price of butcher-meat was low, cattle were expensive to keep, and those who owned them were glad to sell.

The harvest in 1801 was considered a good one, and prices fell considerably, oatmeal being 18s. per boll, fiars' price. Perhaps the crop in that year would be considered but a scant one now, for the average of crops now is far higher than it was sixty years ago, —the land, thanks to the labour and expense that has been expended on it, being much more fruitful than it was then. Public thanksgivings were offered up in the churches for the favourable harvest which it had pleased

God to bestow on His creatures. Oatmeal was only 16s., fiars' price, per boll in 1802.

In the year 1803, when the war with France broke out afresh, after a short interval, there was great excitement in this quarter, and which continued for several years. There was balloting for the militia, not only at first in raising a whole regiment in the county, but every now and then there was balloting to make up losses occasioned by death and by militiamen volunteering into the regiments of the line. The liability to the ballot was extended from eighteen to forty-five years of age. Bodily ailment, of course, was a sufficient cause of exemption; moreover, a married man with three children under ten years of age, and not having property of the value of £100 sterling, was also exempted. A great proportion of those who were liable entered into a society, for the purpose of procuring substitutes for those of their number who might happen to be balloted. The bounties to those substitutes ran very high—from £30 to £40 was frequently given, and we believe that far larger sums were given occasionally. Besides the militia, there was also occasional balloting for what was termed "The Army of Reserve." Then there was the Volunteers; a regiment being raised in this district, Pathhead and St Clairtown furnished its company. Of course the Volunteers were exempted from the ballot, and hence there was no difficulty in filling up the ranks of that corps. Every summer they were turned out for regular service, and marched away to another district of the country—for instance, the Kirkcaldy regiment going to St Andrews one season, to Dunfermline the next, &c., and the regiments belonging to these districts shifting about in the same manner. In 1808 the title "Volunteers" was

changed to that of "Local Militia." This was merely a
change of name, there was no other material difference.
Besides the balloting and volunteering, there were recruiting parties in all parts of the county, belonging
to the various regiments of the line, beating up for
recruits. And connected with all this balloting and recruiting, the minds of the people of this country were
kept in a continual state of ferment by the reports
which were circulated about an invasion by Napoleon
Bonaparte ; and this state of alarm was industriously
laid hold of by the recruiting parties, in their endeavours to induce young men to enlist. Thus we remember distinctly that in 1803, just sixty years ago,
there was a recruiting party stationed in Kirkcaldy
belonging to the Scots Greys. They had large bills
posted up in various public places, setting forth the
great honours and privileges which individuals would
be put in possession of who enlisted in their regiment.
One of these large bills was posted up on the east
corner of that house near the City of Glasgow Bank,
which was for a number of years occupied as a toy
shop ; in this bill there was the most exciting language
about what the French would do *if* they succeeded in
effecting a landing on our shores. It was asserted that
they would " spread rape, rapine, and misery through
this happy land;" and concluding with what was intended
to be a spirit-stirring call, " Now is the time, now or
never, my lads, to shew that free-born Britons never
will be slaves " However, the battle of Trafalgar,
on 21st October 1805, wherein the French and Spanish
fleets were so completely defeated by Lord Nelson, who
lost his life on that eventful day, tended in a great
measure to allay the panic about a French invasion.

The year 1815 was remarkable for great events, in

which not only this country, but almost every country in Europe, was interested. On the 18th of June the great and eventful battle of Waterloo was fought, wherein many thousands of brave men fell belonging to various countries. Among other important consequences that followed it, not the least was the peace which was settled between our own country and France, " our natural enemy," as she has been very foolishly called, and which has now continued uninterrupted for a period of forty-eight years, and which we hope will still continue—yea, continue for ever. That year was remarkable for the great internal prosperity which existed in this country, and in this district particularly. Trade was brisk, and particularly the linen manufacture, and wages were good. Besides, provisions were cheap— the Fife fiars' price of oatmeal being 14s., the lowest rate which has been recorded since 1788, when it was only 12s. But the following year, 1816, brought about a mournful change of matters. The weather was backward, and the harvest consequently scant—meal being £1, 7s. 2d.; in 1817, £1, 7s. Besides, the linen manufacture in this neighbourhood came almost to a dead stand, and great suffering was the consequence. The writer was present at a meeting of the inhabitants of Pathhead and St Clairtown, (and a full one it was,) in what is now termed Dunnikier Church, about the month of October, assembled for the purpose of contributing a mite each to prevent a few families from dying of famine. This meeting consisted exclusively of those who were suffering themselves. A plate was handed round, but the collection consisted of copper; there was one piece of silver; we are not aware that there was any more. But trade began to revive a little in 1817, and the harvests also began to revive gradually;

so that in 1819 the boll of oatmeal was 16s. 6d. fiars' price.

The years 1825 and 1826 deserve a short notice here, being rather out of the ordinary course of years. The former was remarkable for an immense amount of speculation. A very great number of joint-stock companies were formed, and more capital was subscribed towards them than existed at the time in Great Britain. But 1826 overturned nine-tenths of these schemes, the few that were persevered in never prospered, and many individuals were ruined in consequence, for a remarkable dulness of trade took place through the whole country. But the year 1826 was remarkable for another circumstance—Scotland was burned up with drought. Scarce a shower fell from April until the crops were cut down. The quality of the grain was excellent, but the crops of all kinds were remarkably short, with the exception of wheat, which was a good crop. There was very little straw. In many places the oats were not much more than a foot high, and were, as well as beans, pulled up by the roots, instead of being cut down. There was a great scarcity of water in almost every place. In Kirkcaldy, particularly, there was a great want of that necessary of life; for this was before the supply had been obtained from beyond the bounds of the town. The mill leads were, many of them, totally unfit to move the machinery, so that the few steam-mills that then existed were well employed.

In the year 1828 the feuars purchased a garden at the north of the burying-ground, from the heirs of the late John Robertson, for the purpose of taking a portion of it to add to the burying-ground. They paid a very high price for it—namely, £380; but, in addition, there were arrears of feu-duty, lawyers' and other expenses. It was a very dear bargain. One-fifth was converted into burying-ground, and the remaining four-fifths were sold to Mr David Bogie for £158, 10s., in 1835. Taking into account its aggregate cost, and deducting what was received for it at last, and the rents during the short period the feuars had it in their possession, there must have been a dead loss of £350 or upwards, besides the interest of the original pur-chase-money, which lay as a dead weight on the feuars for a number of years afterwards. However, it must be noted that, on the other hand, the feuars have in possession, of course, the addition to the burying-ground, which they sell in lots of £1 each.

In 1846 the poor-law was adopted by the inhabi-tants of the parish of Dysart. For some time previous very strenuous efforts were made by some individuals in the parish to supply the wants of the poor and needy by means of a voluntary contribution, and thus prevent the necessity of having recourse to a com-pulsory assessment. In particular, the late Mr David Murray, the first minister, deserved great praise for the part he acted in regard to this matter. He went round personally through the parish, and gathered up a volun-tary contribution; but it would not do. The benevo-lent gave willingly, but there was no power to compel the selfish. So the voluntary scheme had to be aban-doned, and the compulsory one adopted; and so all are reached now, willing or unwilling. A union poor-house has been erected at Thornton, for the parishes of Dysart, Wemyss, Markinch, and Leslie. It was opened in 1862.

In the beginning of this century the feuars of Path-head, unfortunately, but unavoidably, got into debt; and instead of getting gradually relieved from this burden, they kept sinking deeper and deeper, until,

about the years 1832 and 1833, their debt amounted
to about £500. This accumulation of debt arose from
various causes. There was the old school-house, which,
although it did not cost them much at first, yet was a
very expensive affair to the very end; the purchase of
the garden, of which we have already spoken; the
erection of the Town-Hall and Lock-up; law expenses
connected with Jock's Road; defence against the ex-
action of teinds, &c. But we are happy to have it in
our power to record, that, by dint of persevering
economy and good management, the whole of this debt
was liquidated by the month of June 1852, when the
treasurer announced to the annual general meeting that,
instead of any debt standing against the feuars, as had
been the case for half a century previous, there was at
that time £25 in his hands. And, be it remarked,
that, during all the time when the debt was being paid
off, improvements were going on, less or more, in the
farm, and also in the streets, &c., in the town, principally paid from the public funds of the feuars.
And since that period they have had the good sense to
keep entirely out of debt.

## POPULATION.

| | PATHHEAD. | | PARISH OF DYSART. |
|---|---|---|---|
| 1755 | ... —— | ............ | 2367 |
| 1791 | ... —— | ............ | 4862 |
| 1801 | ... —— | ............ | 5385 |
| 1811 | ... 1692 | ............ | 5506 |
| 1821 | ... —— | ............ | 6429 |
| 1831 | ... 2090 | ............ | 7114 |
| 1841 | ... —— | ............ | —— |
| 1851 | ... 2335 | ............ | 8724 |
| 1861 | ... 2393 | ............ | 8794 |

# APPENDIX.

No. I.

## THE LANDS OF HAWKHEAD MILLS.

WE have already said that the town of Pathhead is bounded on the west by the lands of Hawkhead Mills and the Holmes. Various references are made in the burgh books of Dysart to this property. It appears to have derived its name simply from the fact that it belonged to a family of the name of Hawkhead or Halket for several generations,—a name which is still to be found in this neighbourhood. Under date of 1595, occurs this entry, " James Halkheid his sasing sax akaris land in the north syde of Halkheids malting barne." It would appear, from the extent of land mentioned in this entry, that the Holmes were included with the Hawkhead lands. Again, in 1601, we find " Archibald halkheid son to umqhile James Halkheid ;" " halkheid's myll " is also mentioned. In 1609, again " halket's mill beside the east brig of Kirkaldy." In 1628, " David Simson, miller at halket's mylne." It thus appears that a mill stood on the south-west corner of the land, not very far from the east bridge of Kirkcaldy, and must have been driven by a small stream of water which comes out of the brae, and which is considerably higher than the burn, and which still runs through the property of Robert Hutchison, Esq., and

which finds its way out of the wall two or three yards
east from the bridge. Steam was not thought of then for
any purpose, and the mill could not have been driven
by the burn, which is far too low for that purpose.

In the latter half of last century the *lower* portion of
these lands, with the Holmes, came into the possession
of Cowan & Co., who erected a brewery there, but
which, in the last decade of the century, was converted
into a distillery by the Messrs Spears, who also built
the very respectable-looking dwelling-house near the
east bridge. After passing through the hands of various proprietors in the same line, it was purchased by
the present proprietor, Robert Hutchison, Esq., who
has converted the property into a flour and meal steam-
mill and granary. Mr Hutchison had some time previously purchased the *upper* portion of Hawkhead lands,
which is now denominated " Braehead." He has also
lately made a purchase of the Holmes, so that now the
whole property belongs to one individual, as two hundred years ago. It holds of the Earl of Rothes.
Braehead House, the mansion of Robert Hutchison, is
a very respectable building. It stands about one
hundred yards west from the west end of Mid Street.
It was built by the late Mr Robert Mitchel, somewhere
about the year 1795, the then proprietor of the upper
portion of the lands of Hawkhead Mills. Mr Mitchel
was a very remarkable character. He was born in the
parish of Largo, we were almost going to say, but the
truth is, *he was not born*, but came into the world by
means of the Cæsarian operation. He was brought up
in that neighbourhood, and when he grew up, he became
a labourer, working at road-making, ditching, &c. He
was considerably above the ordinary size, and was
possessed of great strength and activity, and was

understood to have generally performed the work of *two* ordinary men. When he was a young man he paid a visit to the north of England, and taking a stroll into a certain town there on the day of a fair, he was accosted by a bully, who challenged him to fight. But although Mr Mitchel was a very powerful man, he was by no means quarrelsome, but very quiet and peaceable. As the bully kept molesting him, he told him repeatedly that he had no inclination to fight, but when, at last, he saw that he could not get quit of the fellow by fair means, he took hold of him by *the cuff of the neck,* as we say in Scotland, and fairly threw him over the heads of the people who were standing around. Of course he was not troubled with any more molestation from that quarter. Mr Mitchel became an undertaker for constructing and repairing roads, &c., and was, in course of time, appointed road-surveyor in the Kirkcaldy district, and was at one period factor to James Townsend Oswald, Esq. He was captain of the Pathhead and St Clairtown company of Volunteers, which was raised in 1803. As we have already said, he became proprietor of the property of Braehead, and built the mansion-house; but the house has been enlarged and embellished by the present proprietor, Robert Hutchison, Esq., and all the grounds in the vicinity of the house have been put in the most beautiful and ornamental order by him. We may also add, in conclusion, that in digging for the purpose of making improvements, a few yards west from the house, a few years ago, there were several stone coffins or cists found, some of them containing skulls and other human bones; as also a cup of very curious composition, and which is carefully preserved by Mr Hutchison. These remains are supposed to be older than the Christian era.

## No. II.

## ST CLAIRTOWN AND RAVENSCRAIG CASTLE.

ST CLAIRTOWN is virtually a suburb of Pathhead, and has unquestionably sprung out of it. We have already remarked, in the body of our work, that the situation of Pathhead is such, that it cannot be extended either to the east or the west. It extends the whole breadth of Dunnikier estate on its southern extremity. St Clairtown actually joins its three principal streets on the east; on the west it is completely shut in by the lands of Hawkhead Mills, upper and lower, and the sea is its southern boundary; of course there can be no addition made to it in that direction. And, moreover, if we turn our attention to its northern boundary, namely, the arable lands of Dunnikier, we are virtually shut out, for modern feu-duties are entirely out of the question with any individual except wealthy manufacturers or retired merchants, or such like. If then any of the inhabitants of Pathhead, who might have realised a little money, entertained the wish of erecting a house for himself and family in the vicinity of his native place, he had no resource but to betake himself to St Clairtown, where, until of late years, the feus were reasonable. Hence we actually find that the great proportion of the inhabitants of St Clairtown are descended from those who in former days were domiciled in Pathhead.

We cannot speak positively about the period when St Clairtown began to be feued. Whether any houses were erected on it previous to the eighteenth century, we cannot say, but there certainly were a few houses built in the locality in the early part of it; we par-

ticularly allude to that portion of it which forms a con-
tinuation of the Mid Street of Pathhead and old Shuttle-
field, which last has of late years been put out of
existence, in order to make room for the spacious
warehouses, &c., of the Messrs Speedie. We are,
moreover, quite certain, that the great proportion of
the houses in St Clairtown have been built since 1780.
There are no *private* buildings in the whole district
worthy of notice. In general, they are comfortable
dwelling-houses for that class who erected them—
namely, working men—and are generally superior to
the great proportion of the old houses in Pathhead.
The public buildings consist of the two places of worship—namely, the Established and Free Churches, of
which we have already spoken, and the School at the
upper end, which was built wholly by private subscriptions and donations, without any assistance being
requested from Government; and farther, and the only
other building that demands our attention, is Ravenscraig Castle.

Ravenscraig Castle stands on a precipitous rock on
the southwest corner of St Clairtown, and of the estate
of the Earl of Rosslyn. It appears to have been separated, in ancient times, from the adjacent ground by a
deep cut, crossed by a drawbridge, and, before artillery
was invented, would be quite safe from any attack
on the land side ; and the buildings occupying the whole
breadth of the top of the rock, which is perpendicular
on both its east and west sides, it would be also safe
in these directions. On the side next the sea, it could
be quite easily defended from any enemy. A better
spot could not have been selected in ancient times for
the erection of an impregnable castle. All the historians who have referred to it, declare that it is of very

ancient date, but they also all agree in this, that it is impossible to tell when, and by whom it was built.

It was in ancient times a royal castle, although the kings did not reside permanently in it, but only occasionally occupied it when they happened to cross the Forth. At a very remote period, the family of St Clair had intermarried with the royal family of Denmark, and had by this means acquired the earldom of Orkney. King James III. having a strong desire to obtain possession of this earldom, in the year 1470 made an offer to Sir William St Clair of the castle and lands of Ravenscraig, in exchange for it, which was accepted by him, and it is worthy of note that a younger branch of the family of St Clair has been in possession ever since. The succession has not always indeed been in the direct line. Thus, we find that Henry, Master of St Clair, died before his father in 1589, and thus never became Lord St Clair; but he had married Isobel, daughter of the Earl of Rothes, by whom he had three sons, each of whom, in succession, became Lord St Clair. We shall have occasion to notice similar instances before we finish this sketch.

On the 13th February 1592, the Earl of Murray, commonly called "the bonnie Earl of Murray," was cruelly murdered at his seat of Donibristle, by the Earl of Huntly. Two different accounts of this bloody deed are given by historians. Some hold out that the perpetration of this murder was the contrivance of Huntly himself, who, in private revenge and malice, took the opportunity, when he crossed the Forth from Edinburgh, to attack his castle, setting fire to it, and pursuing him as he was fleeing from the burning pile towards the sea, overtook him and killed him. Others again assert that Huntly was only an instrument employed by King James VI., who was jealous of Murray being too familiar with his Queen, Anne of Denmark. But all agree that Huntly and his servants committed the foul deed.

When the tragedy was finished, the Earl of Huntly came east along the coast of Fife, and called at Ravenscraig Castle, asking for shelter, when he was answered by Lord St Clair, (this was the father of the Master of St Clair, to whom we have referred above,) that he was welcome, but that if he had passed by, he would have been twice welcome. Whether Huntly informed him, when he asked for shelter, of the bloody deed in which he had been engaged, we are unable to say.

The family of St Clair continued to reside in Ravenscraig Castle until the period of Cromwell's invasion of Scotland, in the middle of the seventeenth century, when it is said that the English troops dismantled some of the fortifications, and so otherwise injured the buildings that it was no longer fit for the family to reside in. We believe that it was inhabited after that period by some of the retainers of the family, and by other parties, but at present, although still a substantial ruin, which may stand for many ages yet, as a monument of the skill and industry of individuals who lived many centuries back, yet is altogether unfit to be inhabited without a previous outlay of several thousand pounds.

In 1715, John, the Master of St Clair, engaged in the Rebellion, and was attainted by Act of Parliament, and fled to Holland, but in 1726 he obtained a pardon so far as the estates were concerned, but the title went to another branch of the family living in another part of the country. About 1735 he returned home. However, his father, Lord St Clair, previous to the pardon being granted, devised the estate to his second son, James, but he, when his brother returned from exile, generously gave up the estates to him. John dying in 1750, without issue, his brother James succeeded him. James was in the army, and obtained the rank of Colonel in 1722, was Major-General in 1741; he was Lieutenant-General in 1745, and General in 1761. General St Clair was chosen M.P. for the Dysart District of Burghs in 1722, again in 1727, and was returned a third time in 1745. In 1736, he represented the county of Sutherland, and in 1741, and again in 1754, and once afterwards, was chosen for the county of Fife. He died at Dysart in 1762.

General St Clair was succeeded in the possession of the Dysart and Ravenscraig estates by Colonel James Paterson, being the son of the General's sister, the Hon. Grizzel St Clair, and John Paterson, Esq., of Prestonhall. He immediately assumed the name of St Clair. He appears to have been very reasonable and good-humoured. When he was one time personally on the spot granting feus in St Clairtown, somewhere opposite to where the Free Church now stands, after the ground was measured off he said to the feuars, " Now, if you think that you would be better of having a bit more ground, now is the time to speak." Of course they made answer that they would be no worse of a little more. He immediately took his long staff, such as was in fashion in those days, and measured off twice its length of ground in addition to what had been previously marked off. There was an individual of the same name as the Colonel who lived in Pathhead—namely, James Paterson; he was a weaver by trade, but was often employed in sweeping chimneys, and hence was sometimes denominated

Sootie Jamie. He was a very talkative individual, and very ready in quoting Scripture and making ludicrous applications of it in order to make people laugh. He one day got hold of the Colonel, and thus addressed him,—" They call you Jamie Paterson, and me Jamie Paterson—there is nae odds there; they ca' you Colonel St Clair, and me Sootie Jamie—there's a great odds there; but if I gang to heaven and you gang to hell, there will be a greater odds there." We have not heard what reply the Colonel made to this address, if he made any. This eccentric individual died in 1792. The impression on our mind is, that he fell from the roof of a house when engaged in his vocation, and was killed. The Colonel died in 1789.

He was succeeded by Sir James Erskine, grandson to Catherine St Clair, sister to General St Clair. He, like his predecessor, took the name of St Clair; but in 1805 he succeeded to the title of Earl of Rosslyn. He was a general in the army, colonel of the 9th dragoons, a Councillor of State, Director of Chancery in Scotland, and Lord-Lieutenant of the county of Fife. He died in 1837, and was succeeded by his son, the present Earl.

In September 1779, Ravenscraig Castle was occupied as a watch-house. Paul Jones had made his appearance in the mouth of the Firth, and as his name had struck terror into the minds of the inhabitants of the sea-coasts in the country generally, so, when it was announced that he was in such near proximity to this neighbourhood, the people became much alarmed, and a night-watch was appointed, their head-quarters being the castle. A number of young men took it in turns to watch; and it was a piece of service which the young women of the district rendered to the cause, to go down every evening a number of them and put on a good fire for the accommodation of the watchers. We had this relation a few years ago from a female who in her early days was thus engaged.

The castle is shut up the whole year round, with the exception of Handsell Monday, when it is duly opened ; and not only do a number of the inhabitants of Pathhead and St Clairtown visit it, but, if it should happen to be a fine day, numbers of individuals from Kirkcaldy, and even from Abbotshall, may be seen wending their way towards it, just to have it to say that they have seen the castle.   However, we may mention that every Handsell Monday there are a few individuals who make it their business to resort to it for the purpose of engaging in certain games.

THE END.